An Evidence-Centered Approach to Accomplished Teaching

The National Board for Professional Teaching Standards, Inc. has been funded, in part, with grants from the U.S. Department of Education and the National Science Foundation. Through September 2007, NBPTS has been appropriated federal funds of $167.7 million, of which $151.9 million was expended. Such amount represents approximately 32 percent of the National Board's total cumulative costs. Approximately $325.6 million (68 percent) of the National Board's costs were financed by non-federal sources.

The contents of this publication were developed in whole or in part under a grant from the U.S. Department of Education. However, those contents do not necessarily represent the policy of the Department of Education, and you should not assume endorsement by the Federal Government.

ISBN 0-88685-383-4

Printed in the United States of America.

07 06 05 04 03 02 10 9 8 7 6 5 4 3 2 1

Table of Contents

STAGE 3: IMPLEMENT

STAGE 4: ANALYZE & INTERPRET

STAGE 5: REFLECT & APPLY

CONCLUSION

APPENDICES

NOTES

Preface

Welcome and thank you for choosing *Take One!*®: An Evidence-Centered Approach to Accomplished Teaching. You are about to engage in a meaningful, challenging, and rewarding professional development experience.

The National Board for Professional Teaching Standards® (NBPTS®) specifically designed *Take One!* to offer the education community an opportunity to experience a portion of one of the most complex standards-based performance assessments in the field of education today—the assessment leading to National Board Certification®. This assessment has been proven by independent research to contribute to the improvement of teacher quality, which in turn, impacts improved student learning.

At the same time and for over a decade, this nationally respected assessment program routinely earns high praise from teachers and school counselors from across America during their pursuit of National Board Certification. Among the testimonials:

> *"Since going through the National Board Certification process, my teaching has never been the same. It's an empowering professional development program that values what is important in classroom teaching."*
>
> – Laura Johnson, Colorado

> *"The National Board Certification process made me a better teacher. I will probably teach longer because I learned so much about how to expand my practice. I've never had a professional development experience as powerful."*
>
> – John York, North Carolina

> *"The National Board Certification process is the greatest professional development a teacher can go through. I have never worked with any candidate for certification who didn't say it was the best and most effective agent of change for improved student learning. It makes you take a look at everything in the classroom and reflect upon it. It's an opportunity to push yourself and help your students succeed."*
>
> – Elizabeth Anne Rose, Washington

These kinds of commendations have long been heard by NBPTS as the organization works to certify accomplished teachers through its rigorous, standards-based assessment of teaching practice. Now educators at every level, including those in higher education, as well as administrators across the country, have an opportunity to sample a slice of this powerful and respected program.

By choosing *Take One!* you have made the right professional development choice.

Acknowledgements

The National Board for Professional Teaching Standards and Educational Testing Service wish to acknowledge the following individuals who assisted with the development of this publication:

Katherine Bassett
Joseph Ciofalo
Annette DeLuca
Stephanie Epp, NBCT
Patrice Faison, NBCT
Nancy Flanagan, NBCT
Lynn Gaddis, NBCT
Mary Lease, NBCT
Joyce Loveless, NBCT
David Lussier, NBCT
Elizabeth Marquez
Carol Moyer, NBCT
Cathy Owens, NBCT
Misty Sato, NBCT
Steve Schreiner, NBCT
Maria Telesca, NBCT
Cynthia Tocci
Robin Ventura, NBCT

This Activity Book uses information from numerous publications and resources previously published by the National Board for Professional Teaching Standards (NBPTS) and Educational Testing Service (ETS). More information can be found on ***www.nbpts.org*** and ***www.ets.org*** or by accessing the sources cited throughout the Activity Book, which are referenced in the Notes section beginning on page 91.

In addition, the organizations wish to extend a special note of appreciation to Marie Collins who combined all our ideas to write this book.

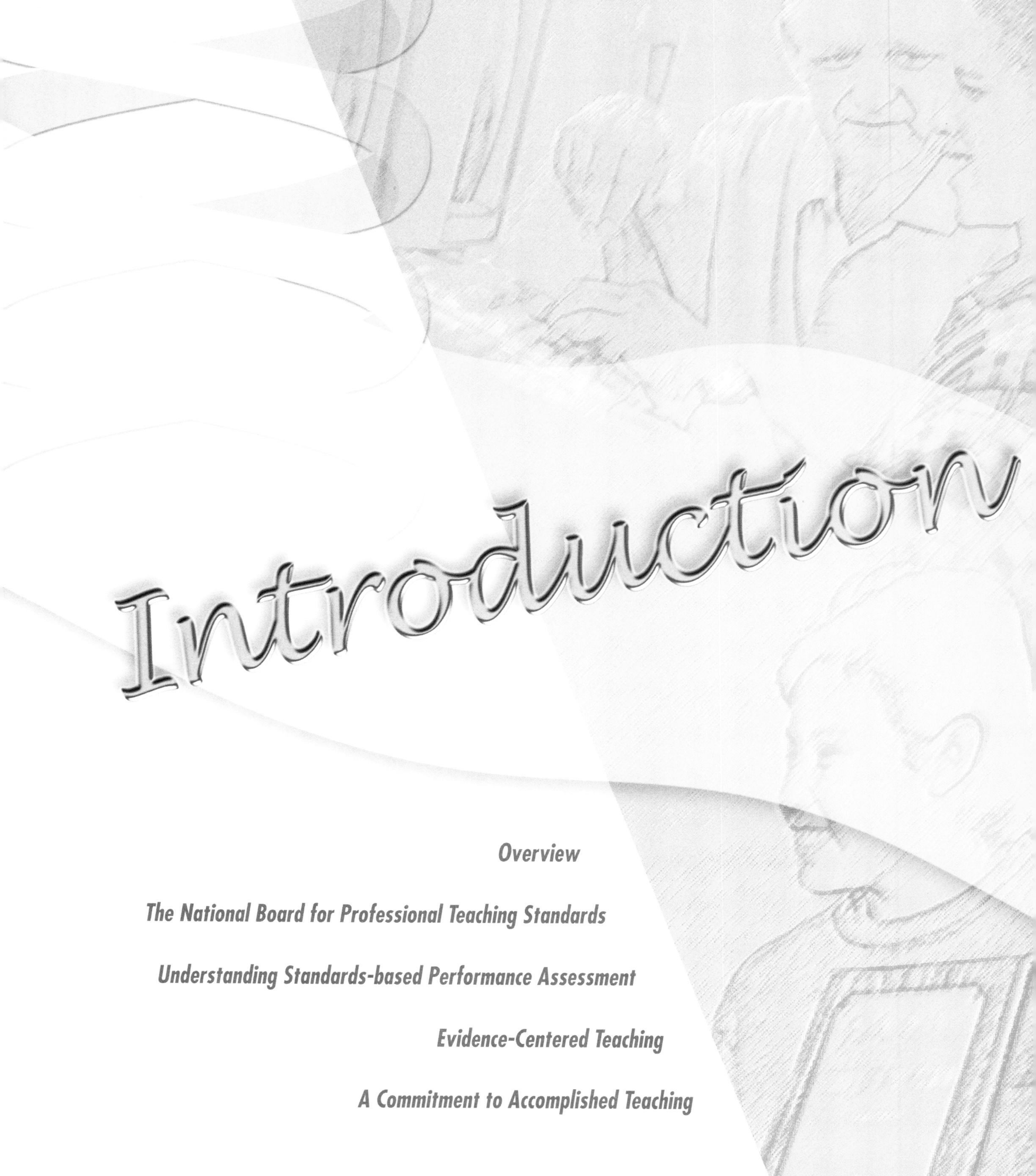

Introduction

Overview

The National Board for Professional Teaching Standards

Understanding Standards-based Performance Assessment

Evidence-Centered Teaching

A Commitment to Accomplished Teaching

Overview

About NBPTS and National Board Certification®

The National Board for Professional Teaching Standards (NBPTS) is a private, nonprofit organization governed by a board of directors, the majority of whom are classroom teachers. The National Board's mission is to maintain high and rigorous standards for what accomplished teachers should know and be able to do; to provide a national voluntary system certifying teachers who meet these standards; and to advocate related education reforms to integrate National Board Certification in American education as well as to capitalize on the expertise of National Board Certified Teachers (NBCTs®).

The National Board Certification process is an unprecedented effort to reshape the public's perception of teaching, to create more professional and educationally rewarding relationships among teachers, to advance the knowledge base of teaching, and to improve student learning. Unlike current, mandatory systems of state licensing, which set entry-level requirements for beginning teachers, National Board Certification is a voluntary process developed by teachers and other education stakeholders to recognize experienced teachers for the quality of their practice. National Board Certification signifies that a teacher is accomplished, having met challenging professional teaching standards as evidenced by performance-based assessments.

During National Board Certification, teachers spend a year documenting and demonstrating their knowledge and skills as professional educators. Each candidate's performance is individually evaluated by expert teachers and judged against the highest standards set by the profession. National Board Certification requires teachers to:

- **assemble portfolios** that include video recorded samples of their teaching practice and that demonstrate their ability to teach subjects effectively, to manage students, to measure student learning, and to
- **complete a series** of rigorous computer-delivered assessment exercises to demonstrate their content knowledge.

Becoming a National Board Certified Teacher requires an investment of time that typically spans the course of a school year while the candidate conducts an in-depth, reflective examination of their teaching practice. To be successful, a candidate must take an honest look at his or her teaching practice in order to evaluate both its strengths and weaknesses. Whether or not they become certified, most identify this process as one that has helped them become better, more effective teachers.[1]

What Can I Expect from *Take One!*?

Take One! is a meaningful and relevant professional development experience that will help you combine the architecture of accomplished teaching practice with an evidence-centered approach to analyzing your impact in the classroom. As you know, teachers usually talk about their practice in terms of what their students are doing rather than what their students are learning. *Take One!* has been designed to bridge the gap between these two important, but different, outcomes.

Using this personal activity book along with your *Take One!* portfolio entry, you can practice and self-assess evidence-centered teaching through reflective analysis. Once you establish clearer connections between how your students learn and how you teach, you should be able to generate more convincing evidence of your effectiveness and make better instructional decisions. This is how accomplished teachers improve student learning.

Take One! can also be a valuable tool to help build instructional capacity in schools by exposing teachers to the professional teaching standards of NBPTS. Whether as a component of a university preparation program for teachers-in-training, one element of a mentoring program for new teachers, or incorporated into a district-wide professional development plan, *Take One!* is a cost-effective way to introduce teachers to standards-based instruction and the elements of accomplished teaching that will help them succeed in the classroom.

Take One! is designed to be a cost-effective, job-embedded, and ongoing professional development experience that helps build learning communities in schools and strengthen professional collaboration among educators. Indeed, *Take One!* provides a platform for groups of educators to work together toward common goals in ways that can enhance both teaching practice and student learning. It is expected that school-wide discussions about student learning will be elevated and integrated collaborations will be fostered as work done in isolation is reduced.

Once you establish clearer connections between how your students learn and how you teach, you should be able to generate more convincing evidence of your effectiveness and make better instructional decisions.

Particularly because of its association with the highly praised NBPTS assessment program, *Take One!* could be a valuable experience for anyone planning to continue the National Board Certification process. It provides insight into the level of work involved, how responses are scored, and how evidence of accomplished teaching is generated, and therefore could be helpful to you in determining your readiness to make a commitment to the remaining process at a given point in time. Keep in mind, however, that successful completion of *Take One!* should not be seen as an indicator for assuring the success of any candidate who pursues National Board Certification.

The National Board for Professional Teaching Standards

Before beginning *Take One!,* one of your most important initial tasks is to thoroughly and carefully study what the NBPTS Standards articulate about effective teaching practice in your content area, with a goal of understanding how they might be reflected in your actual day-to-day practice. All NBPTS Standards are based on the Five Core Propositions that first appeared in the National Board's policy statement *What Teachers Should Know and Be Able To Do.* These propositions define the "knowledge, skills, dispositions, and commitments" of teaching, as follows:

1. Teachers are committed to students and their learning.
2. Teachers know the subjects they teach and how to teach those subjects to students.
3. Teachers are responsible for managing and monitoring student learning.
4. Teachers think systematically about their practice and learn from experience.
5. Teachers are members of learning communities.

As part of *Take One!,* you will be asked to relate what the standards mean in the context of your curriculum and classroom. Simply restating the standards will not fulfill this requirement; rather, you must interpret and apply the standards in terms of your own students and situation, and integrate them into your practice.

Although it is important to review all of the NBPTS Standards, pay particular attention to those standards that serve as the basis for *Take One!.* You will find these standards in abbreviated form on the NBPTS Web site at ***www.nbpts.org/standards/stds.cfm***. Following are some tips and suggestions that can help you become familiar with the standards for your certificate area.[2]

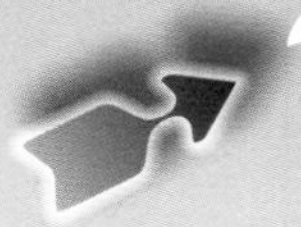

Tips for Studying and Understanding the Standards

1. Look carefully at the Five Core Propositions above that outline what teachers should know and be able to do. Jot down at least one specific act or activity that you and/or your colleagues do regularly that illustrates each proposition.
2. For each standard in the set of standards for your content area/developmental level, ask yourself the following questions:
   - What would an accomplished teacher know and be able to do with respect to this standard? Be very specific.
   - How might an accomplished teacher demonstrate proficiency with respect to this standard? How could such a teacher prove to you that he or she is meeting this standard?
   - What might a teacher do or say that would give convincing evidence that this standard is being met? What is the rationale for that judgment?

The Architecture of Accomplished Teaching

The Architecture of Accomplished Teaching was developed by NBPTS and is a metaphor for what accomplished teachers do in the classroom. Just as two buildings can have very different architectures, they still share common features. Likewise, no two teachers approach their craft in exactly the same manner. However, while individual practices may differ on the surface, all accomplished teachers share fundamental aspects of teaching.

First, accomplished teachers get to know their students and their needs; then they set worthwhile goals that are appropriate for those students. They implement instruction related to those goals, evaluate student learning in connection with the goals, and finally, reflect on student learning in terms of the goals. Once those steps are completed, accomplished teachers begin the process of goal-setting all over again.

The movement from bottom to top within the double helix shown in the Architecture of Accomplished Teaching *(Figure 1)* reflects the accomplished teacher's ongoing processing of student needs, instructional goals, instructional strategies, evaluation, and reflection. Knowledge of students is the basis for any instructional planning; therefore it is the base of the helix. Starting with that knowledge, follow the helix upwards.

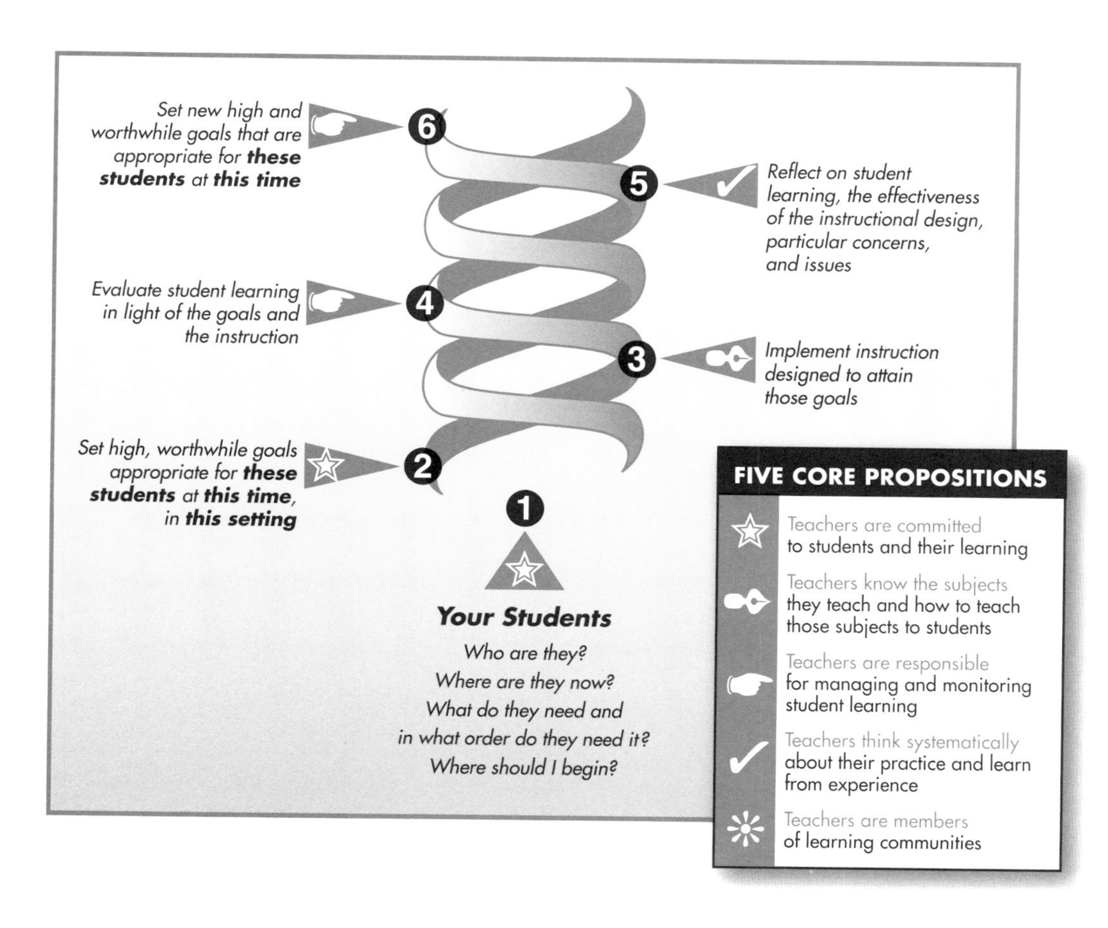

Figure 1
The Architecture of Accomplished Teaching

Understanding Standards-Based Performance Assessment

Standards-based performance tasks require your students to solve or respond to relevant problems or questions, apply key concepts, or demonstrate complex skills—all of which are prescribed in your state and/or district content standards. When you evaluate these performances, you look for evidence that your students have attained the understandings and skills that the standards highlight as important.

Similarly, *Take One!* portfolio entries are standards-based performance tasks. However, in this case, the standards on which the tasks are based are the National Board Standards for professional teaching. That's why your understanding of the standards, as they relate to your curriculum and students, is so important: The portfolio entry you compile must demonstrate your effectiveness in terms of these standards.

National Board Certification

Central to effectively completing your portfolio entry for *Take One!* is the collection and provision of clear, consistent, and convincing evidence of your teaching practices that help your students learn. The pieces of your portfolio entry follow the Architecture of Accomplished Teaching. You begin by demonstrating that you know and understand your students and their learning needs, then show that you select content standards and learning goals that are appropriate and meaningful for those students. Next, you demonstrate your ability to plan a lesson that is closely related to those standards and goals, and is tailored to your students' learning needs. In addition, you compile evidence that your classroom environment encourages student learning and you video record your implementation of the lesson. Finally, you analyze in writing what took place during your teaching, and also reflect on how what you learned about yourself as a teacher and your practice will influence both your future teaching and future student learning.

You begin by demonstrating that you know and understand your students and their learning needs, then show that you select content standards and learning goals that are appropriate and meaningful for those students.

What is "Good Evidence?"

To compile a successful portfolio entry, you are going to have to make some thoughtful decisions about which evidence to include in your entry. Traditionally, teachers have been taught to talk about teaching in terms of behavioral objectives and what they want students to *do* rather than what they want students to *learn*. *Take One!* helps to bridge this gap by emphasizing the need for strong connections between what students are intended to learn, what teachers do to facilitate that learning, and what students do that demonstrates they have actually achieved that learning. As *Figure 2* shows, "good evidence" of effective teaching sits at the nexus between what teachers and students do; it shows how effective teaching helps students learn.

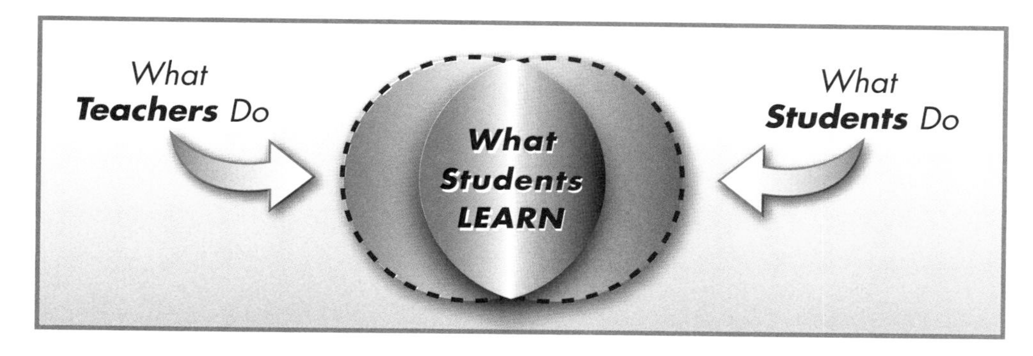

Figure 2
What Makes Good Evidence?

The *Take One! Activity Book* offers information and activities that can help you produce and collect evidence of what you do in your daily teaching practice. The focus of this activity book—and *Take One!*—is a video entry; however, the skills and processes described in this activity book can help you complete other portfolio entries as well. For example, three of four portfolio entries required for NBPTS certification ask you to provide evidence that you know your students and that you use that knowledge to plan and teach a purposeful lesson that is appropriate for them.

In addition, NBPTS portfolio entries ask you to articulate in writing why aspects of your teaching practice are effective or could be more so. While many teachers feel confident that their instructional practices are successful, they often have difficulty explaining why and how they succeed. Thus, in addition to helping you become more adept at collecting evidence and using it to enhance your teaching, completing this activity book will help provide practice in thinking and writing about your teaching and how it impacts student learning.

At the end of each stage, a note indicates the parts of *Take One!* to which you can apply your work. When you complete the activity book, you may find that you have produced enough "good" evidence to complete *Take One!*. The conclusion offers suggestions to help you evaluate and strengthen your evidence.

Evidence-Centered Teaching

At the core of the Architecture of Accomplished Teaching is evidence-centered teaching—a way of structuring classroom planning and instruction that enables teachers to continuously gather, interpret, and use evidence of student learning to make appropriate daily decisions that determine the course and nature of future instruction. The goal of evidence-centered teaching is to design learning experiences that are coherently aligned with content standards and learning goals, that are meaningful for all students, and that empower all students to effectively demonstrate what they have learned. Evidence, as defined below, is central to the approach.

Evidence

Tangible student outcomes, data, or information (for example, from student participation, discussion, board work, homework, presentations, projects, writing, tests, and so on) that have been identified, collected, interpreted, and used to:

- identify patterns of learning
- support conclusions about a student's knowledge, skills, or other attributes
- influence claims about students' future learning
- provide diagnostic feedback for groups of students as well as individual students

Steps of Evidence-Centered Teaching

At each step of evidence-centered teaching, teachers gather, interpret, and use evidence of their students' ongoing mastery of the content standards to guide their instructional decision-making, as follows:

1. **The teacher makes a claim** about intended student learning (what students will know or be able to do as a result of instruction) that is grounded in state and/or district content standards, evidence of what students already know and can do, particular content, discipline-specific behaviors, an understanding of individual learners, and overall learning goals or outcomes.
2. **The teacher describes the evidence** that will demonstrate that students have indeed accomplished the learning reflected in the claim.
3. **The teacher determines the best instructional vehicle** for capturing the evidence he or she identified and plans a lesson. She or he designs learning activities, selects teaching strategies, and develops assessment tasks to elicit and capture the evidence.
4. **The teacher sets performance criteria** and constructs or adapts a performance rubric to evaluate the depth of the learning that is expected to result from the learning activities and assessments, as reflected in the evidence.

Cycles of Evidence-Centered Teaching

Evidence-centered teaching proceeds cyclically. After step 4, the teacher implements the planned lesson, gathers the needed evidence, and uses that evidence to determine whether students achieved the initial claim. In addition, this evidence provides the basis for future instructional claims, which are made by repeating the cycle.[3]

Figure 3 illustrates the impact of evidence-centered teaching in the classroom. As the arrows throughout the diagram show, reciprocal relationships facilitate coherence among key aspects of the lesson. For instance, the lesson is based on earlier evidence and generates new evidence; evidence both confirms students have achieved a proposed claim and provides the basis for a new one; and a scoring rubric enables the teacher to articulate performance criteria at the heart of the claim, support student learning during the lesson, and later evaluate the resulting evidence in terms of the claim.

Figure 3
Cycles of Evidence-Centered Teaching

Understanding the Nature of Evidence

In completing National Board portfolio entries, it is important to distinguish "evidence" of your teaching effectiveness from descriptions of your teaching practices. Descriptions do not document what students learned; they merely record events or provide your opinions about what could or should be done. Descriptions do not provide information about what students learned as a result of what was done.

To document student learning and the effectiveness of your classroom practice, it is essential to look to evidence that stands independently of descriptions and opinions. Remember, good evidence provides clear, consistent, and convincing proof that your students have indeed learned what you intended them to learn.

A Commitment To Accomplished Teaching

NBPTS is committed to recognizing accomplished teachers and encouraging teachers who may not yet meet the standards of accomplished teaching to move closer to that goal. The National Board believes very strongly that teachers who become more knowledgeable about what and how they teach become better teachers, and that engaging more teachers in self-reflection about their teaching practice improves the quality of both teaching and student learning.

In its continuing effort to measure the impact of National Board Certification and the effects of NBCTs on the quality of teaching and student achievement in America's schools, NBPTS has engaged in an independent, rigorous research agenda. There have been more than 160 studies, reports, and papers commissioned on the value of the National Board Certification process, as well as its standards and assessments.

Research demonstrates that NBCTs help students learn more—measurably raising student performance, achieving particularly notable gains among lower-income students, and driving meaningful changes in their classrooms and throughout their schools. There is a growing body of evidence that National Board Certification is a smart investment in our schools and for our children. Below are highlights of three studies.

November 2004, The CNA Corporation

This research found that students of NBCTs did a measurably better job than other ninth- and tenth-graders on year-end math tests in Miami-Dade County (Fla.) Public Schools.

- All else being equal—student characteristics, school environment, and teacher preparation—Miami-Dade math teachers who had achieved National Board Certification helped their students achieve larger testing gains than did colleagues who had not earned certification.
- The study of more than 100,000 student Florida Comprehensive Assessment Test (FCAT) records found that NBCTs are particularly effective with students who have special needs, and provides some evidence that African-American and Hispanic students may also receive extra benefits.

September 2004, Arizona State University

This research showed that third-, fourth-, fifth-, and sixth-graders taught by NBCTs in 14 Arizona school districts outperformed their schoolmates on the nationwide Stanford Achievement Test 9th Edition (SAT-9) in almost 75 percent of reading, math, and language arts measures.

- On average, students of NBCTs scored as if they had received more than a month's worth of additional instruction.

- In Arizona, which spends nearly $7,000 per year per student, that extra classroom time is the equivalent of almost $1,000 worth of additional learning for each student.
- 85 percent of principals surveyed said NBCTs in their schools were among the best teachers they had ever supervised; 91 percent said they believe National Board Certification helps improve teacher quality.

March 2004, University of Washington/Urban Institute

A U.S. Department of Education-funded multiyear study of more than 600,000 records from third-, fourth-, and fifth-grade students in North Carolina found that:

- Teachers who achieve National Board Certification do a measurably better job in the classroom.
- Students of NBCTs improved an average of 7 percent more on their year-end math and reading tests than students of non-NBCTs.
- This performance differential was most pronounced for younger and lower-income students whose gains were as high as 15 percent.

In addition, working toward National Board Certification:

- offers an enriching professional growth opportunity for experienced teachers
- energizes good teachers and helps keep them engaged in the classroom
- develops accomplished teachers who can serve as mentors to other teachers
- provides schools with a measure of teacher quality

Teachers who complete the National Board Certification process consistently rate it the best professional development experience of their careers.

In less than a decade, all 50 states and more than 500 school districts have recognized the value of National Board Certification by establishing financial or other types of incentives to encourage teachers to go through the process. What's more, teachers who complete the National Board Certification process consistently rate it the best professional development experience of their careers.

Whether you are a classroom teacher, a facilitator, or an educator who works with current or future classroom teachers, we are confident that you will find *Take One!* helpful in gaining insight into accomplished teaching as well as National Board Certification. We commend you for your interest in the National Board's goal of improving teaching and learning.[4]

Stage 1 Identify

Knowledge of Students

Learning Goals

Knowledge of Students

There is a great deal more to good teaching than being well versed in a subject and its related pedagogy. The most effective teachers are also skilled practitioners of the art of getting to know their students and applying that knowledge in ways that help those students become more successful learners. Taking the time to get to know as much as possible about your students—their interests, talents, strengths, concerns, and learning styles, as well as cultural, social, and family influences—can help you plan effective, meaningful lessons that engage and challenge them, and can give you the information you need to assess your students' learning more accurately and in ways that inform your teaching. As a result, students tend to feel more confident in their learning abilities and more motivated to learn.

In other words, in addition to considering the lesson and subject matter being covered, you need to think about your students. What do they already know—or think they know—about the subject? What will they find interesting? Conversely, what will they find downright tedious? How can you make every lesson exciting, relevant, and approachable for your students while still advancing important learning goals? What instructional strategies will help a student who is having particular difficulty with the concepts being covered? To answer these questions, you need to start with the students themselves. You need to find out, to the extent possible:

> **NBPTS Core Proposition 1:**
>
> *Teachers are committed to students and their learning.*

- **where** your students are in terms of their intellectual, social, and emotional development, and whether they have any special learning needs
- **how** they feel most comfortable learning
- **what** they know and what they don't know, what they can do and what they can't do, and whether they have developed any misconceptions that could stand in the way of learning
- **what** they are interested in or passionate about, both in school and outside of school
- **what** their cultural backgrounds are and how these backgrounds may affect how they feel about learning, see the world, participate in learning activities, or absorb new information
- **how** any issues or events taking place in their lives are affecting their attitudes about learning

Stop & Write About Your Practice Now

1. Select the class or group of students with whom you work. Identify the class or group below.

____

____

____

2. For each of the four elements listed below, rate your current proficiency with demonstrating your knowledge of your students. Consider your strengths as well as areas in which you want to improve, then note "basic," "proficient," or "accomplished" next to each element in the list that follows. Be as objective as possible.

Knowledge Rating

Element	Basic	Proficient	Accomplished
Knowledge of Characteristics of This Age Group	☐	☐	☐
Knowledge of Students' Varied Approaches to Learning	☐	☐	☐
Knowledge of Your Students' Skills and Knowledge	☐	☐	☐
Knowledge of Your Students' Interests and Cultural Heritage	☐	☐	☐

3. List the strengths that your self-assessment has revealed, and next to each, provide at least one example from your practice.

Strength	Example
____________	______________________________
____________	______________________________
____________	______________________________
____________	______________________________

4. With which element are you most comfortable? Why?

____

____

____

(continued on next page)

5. With which element are you least comfortable? Why?

6. List the areas in which you would like to improve.

7. In one to three sentences, summarize the manner in which you currently demonstrate knowledge of your students.

8. How does your cultural background influence the way you see the world and participate in learning activities?

9. Recall a time when your background knowledge either positively or negatively affected a learning experience that you were involved in (such as a graduate class, professional seminar, or an adult workshop).

10. How do your own interests and talents influence what and how you learn?

Developing Knowledge of Your Students as Learners

Making information interesting, relevant, and challenging (but not frustrating), and presenting it in such a way that your students can connect with it, is key to engaging students in learning. But students are individuals and, as such, are very different from one another—fundamentally different in how they learn and what they find interesting, meaningful, and worth putting effort into.

What does this mean? It means that successful teaching—teaching that gives each student a chance to learn, a chance to grow, and a chance to succeed—requires more than knowing the material you're teaching or having a diverse repertoire of teaching strategies, approaches, and tools. While these are essential aspects of good teaching, they are ineffective without knowing your students' interests, their aspirations, and how they feel about learning and why. Also, before you can determine which strategies are appropriate or which tools will be most effective, you need to know where your students are in terms of what they know and don't know as it relates to the content they are learning.

You can use your knowledge of your students to respond quickly and effectively to both planned and spontaneous learning opportunities and situations.

Once you have this information, you can use it to inform and guide your lesson plans and activities, as well as your assessment methods. As you become more experienced and comfortable using the knowledge you have of your students, you can use it to help them connect new learning to what they already know or to their interests outside of school, such as hobbies that are of personal interest. Knowing your students can also help you gain an understanding of the learning strategies that are most likely to work best for them. Most of all, you can use your knowledge of your students to respond quickly and effectively to both planned and spontaneous learning opportunities and situations.

Example

A language arts teacher who understands the importance of using what he or she knows about his or her students to plan meaningful learning considers the fact that a specific class of eighth-grade students has a passion for art, drama, and music. As he or she plans a culminating project for a unit on poetry, the teacher decides to tap into this passion by allowing students to show what they've learned about poetry through their choice of a variety of forms of expression: Students may choose to create their own poems, illustrate a poem, give an oral presentation explaining their interpretation of a poem, or present a creative dance or musical interpretation of a poem.

Appendix A: Investigative Tools lists a variety of investigative tools you can use to develop a deeper understanding of your students, and also shows the kind of information each tool can help you unearth. While providing a full explanation of these tools and how to use them is beyond the scope of this activity book, the table points to a resource you can use to learn more.

In the pages that follow, the *Take One! Activity Book* provides information about a sample investigative tool—kidwatching—that you can apply right away.

Sample Investigative Tool: "Kidwatching"

"Kidwatching," a term coined by Yetta Goodman, refers to focused, purposeful observation of students in the act of learning. It's a technique that can reveal a wealth of information about students—information that often can't be learned through formal testing.

For example, kidwatching can help you notice signs—some subtle and some quite obvious—of how your students are handling their learning experiences. You may spot confusion or understanding; identify patterns of behavior and areas of strength or need; get a sense of students' motivation and interest; learn how students approach problems; and observe how students interact with their peers. These observations, in turn, can help you determine who needs help learning as well as how to help.

True kidwatching includes three steps: observation, interaction, and analysis.

You can kidwatch while you circulate among students who are engaged in learning. Or you can plan a kidwatching event by scheduling a time to meet briefly with a student. During this meeting you might have the student read for you while you record ways in which the student's reading deviates from the actual text (a "running record"). Or you might use this time to discuss a piece of student work, such as a writing sample or math problem. The session, although carefully planned, should be low-key, friendly, and brief. A few minutes will do, if you know what you're looking for and carefully plan the questions or tasks that will provide the information you need.

True kidwatching includes three steps: observation, interaction, and analysis. Examples of questions you can ask yourself or your students at each step follow. Also, at each step, keeping a record of your observations, student responses, and your findings—using checklists, time sampling, running records, case studies, or other methods—is key to effective kidwatching.

Step 1: Observation

- What is the student's attitude toward the situation, task, or problem?
- What types of activities does the student seem to prefer?
- Does the student relate concepts to real-world situations?

Step 2: Interaction

- What are you exploring? What are you reading?
- What information do you need to know to solve this problem? How can you get this information?
- What do you think will happen next? Can you tell me more?
- Have you discussed this problem (or this book, reading) with anybody else? Will you tell me about that discussion?

Step 3. Analysis

- What types of materials does the student read? What task or problem is he or she exploring?
- Are the students' retellings, summaries, or reading/task sequential in nature? Is attention given to pertinent details and concepts?
- Is the student's vocabulary or conceptual knowledge growing?
- How does the student behave during periods of transition?

It's Your Turn

Directions: Now that you have reconsidered the importance of knowing your students, complete this activity to learn more about your particular students.

1. Select three students who present different teaching challenges for you to be the focus of both your efforts to deepen your knowledge of your students and *Take One!*. Write their names in columns 1, 2, and 3 of the ***Investigative Tools Checklist***, which follows; in the space marked "Rationale," briefly note why you are investigating each student.

2. Use the Investigative Tools Checklist to select a few tools for collecting information about each of the students you identified; in columns 1, 2, and 3, note the different tools you will use to learn about each one. If necessary, learn more about the tools you selected.

3. Note what you need to do to use each tool you have chosen. For example, you may need to determine whom you will speak with and what you will ask, or which records to review and how to obtain them. As you plan, keep your rationale in mind.

4. Apply the tools you selected to gather information about your students.

5. Sort, analyze, and interpret the information you collected to deepen your understanding of each student you identified. As you analyze, keep in mind the rationale you used to structure your investigation.

You will have a chance to apply what you learned about these students later in the activity book, when you plan, video record, and evaluate a lesson for *Take One!*. The evidence of student learning that you collect during your lesson should help you understand how your new knowledge influenced your students' learning.

Investigative Tools Checklist*

Name of Student:	**1.**	**2.**	**3.**
Rationale for Investigation:			
People			
☐ Colleagues			
☐ Guidance counselors			
☐ Administrators			
☐ Social worker			
☐ Nurse			
☐ Psychologist			
☐ Other educational professionals			
☐ Family members and/or other adult caregivers			
☐ Coaches			
☐ Student			
☐ Other ________________			
Records			
☐ Previous report cards			
☐ Portfolios			
☐ Standardized test scores			
☐ Individual Educational Plans (IEPs)			
☐ Cumulative records			
☐ Diagnostic tests			
☐ Reports from experts			
☐ Other records __________			

** For examples of the kind of information these tools can help you unearth, see Appendix A.*

Name of Student:	1.	2.	3.
Other Investigative Tools			
☐ Interest inventory/survey			
☐ Learning-style inventory/survey			
☐ Conference with student			
☐ Conference with parents or other adult caregiver who assumes responsibility for nurturing and caring for this student			
☐ "Kidwatching"			
☐ Informal observations			
☐ Games/classroom activities			
☐ Assignments			
☐ Pretests and posttests			
Other Resources			
☐			
☐			

Next Steps

Knowing who your students are—how they think and learn, what interests them, and how their cultural backgrounds and personal experiences contribute to their classroom learning—is the foundation of effective teaching. Before you as a teacher can answer the question, "How will I know when my students have learned what I want them to learn?" you must first establish a learning goal by asking yourself, "What do I want my students to learn?" And before you can determine what your students should learn, you must identify where they are now.

Think about these questions before you advance to the next section of Stage 1, where you will select the learning goal that will drive the lesson you plan for *Take One!*:

- What knowledge, skills, and abilities *should* my students have before I begin teaching this lesson?
- Do they have these knowledge, skills, and abilities? To what degree? What evidence do I have that shows me this?
- What do I know about my students—such as their interests, attention spans, abilities, needs, learning styles, and more—that can help me select learning goals and instructional methods that are the most appropriate and challenging *for them?*[1]

Learning Goals

Once you have identified the relevant characteristics of your students, it's time to ask yourself what you want to teach these students. At this point you identify:

- the standard(s) to be addressed by the lesson—which can help you define the specific skills and understandings you will teach
- the learning goals and concepts to be taught during the lesson, based on the standard(s) chosen[1]

What is a Learning Goal?

A learning goal is a clear statement of what students will learn as the result of a purposeful, evidence-centered lesson. Learning goals written by accomplished teachers:

- relate strongly to state and/or district content standards
- advance high expectations and worthwhile learning
- specify what students will *learn* rather than what they will *do*
- are clearly worded
- are appropriate for the diverse students for whom they are written (e.g., in terms of age, developmental levels, learning approaches, prior learning, interests, and cultural backgrounds)
- can be achieved with accomplished teaching strategies
- can be measured using classroom-based assessment methods and performance standards

In general, it is a teacher's responsibility to develop the learning goals at the heart of his or her lessons. However, teachers must take into account a number of factors when they establish goals for student learning—such as state and/or district content standards and curriculum, requirements of external mandates (such as AP® exams), and community expectations. In classrooms organized as communities of learners, teachers often engage students in collectively determining learning goals.

Learning goals target specific knowledge and understandings, academic skills, thinking skills, or social skills. Indeed, content and process goals are usually present simultaneously in effective learning goals.

Over time, learning goals should reflect a balance among a variety of types of learning.[2]

Learning Goals Versus Learning Activities

When developing learning goals, it is important to distinguish learning *goals* from learning *activities*. Learning goals state what students will learn as a result of the entire lesson, while learning activities describe any number of things that students will *do* during the lesson to achieve that learning.

To determine whether a statement more clearly represents a learning goal or activity, ask yourself:

- **What** does the statement say the student will be able to do *after* the lesson?
- Is the learning stated in the goal measurable? **How**?[3]

The *table* that follows illustrates the differences between learning goals and activities.

Learning Goals or Activities?	
Learning Goals	**Learning Activities**
Students will:	**Students will:**
• distinguish between words beginning with "p" and "b"	• play bingo using words beginning with "p" and "b"
• determine the electrical conductivity of different materials	• conduct an experiment investigating the electrical conductivity of different materials

Adapted/reprinted with permission from *Framework Observation Program: Participant Guidebook* (p. 45). Princeton, NJ: ETS, 2001. Available: http://www.ets.org/pathwise.

Learning goals state what students will learn as a result of the entire lesson, while learning activities describe any number of things that students will do during the lesson to

Stop & Write About Your Practice Now

A. Learning Goal or Activity?[4] Next to each statement below, indicate whether it is an activity (A) or a learning goal (G). Rewrite as learning goals all statements you marked with an "A." Check your answers in Appendix B: Learning Activities.

_____ 1. Recognize a poem in sonnet form.
_____ 2. Distinguish between different types of triangles.
_____ 3. Read the next chapter and answer the questions.
_____ 4. Identify three major types of water pollution and the causes of each.
_____ 5. Play the game of basketball.
_____ 6. Regroup addition problems involving three-digit numbers.
_____ 7. Determine the quantities of ingredients needed if a recipe is tripled.
_____ 8. Do a science experiment with magnets and batteries.
_____ 9. Explain the factors leading to the Industrial Revolution.
_____ 10. Take a walking field trip to look for signs of autumn.
_____ 11. Complete a worksheet on the Civil War.
_____ 12. Identify the characteristics of living things.
_____ 13. Role-play a conversation between General Washington and his troops at Valley Forge.
_____ 14. Sing harmoniously in a chorus, following the director's lead.
_____ 15. Fill in the blanks on the language arts worksheet.

B. Building Skill with Learning Goals. Think about the learning goals you regularly write for your students. Based on the qualities of effective learning goals (i.e., they state what students will *learn* rather than *do*; they are strongly linked to content standards; they are clear, appropriate, and worthwhile; they advance high expectations; they are attainable using established teaching strategies; and they are measurable), note how you could strengthen them.

____

____

____

____

____

____

It's Your Turn

Directions: Think about the class or students who will be the focus of your *Take One!* submission, as well as what you learned about the three students you identified earlier. In the spaces that follow:

1. Note the Content Standard(s) around which you will develop a lesson for your entry.

2. Write a Learning Goal for the lesson.

3. Under Rationale, explain how the learning goal you developed relates to the standard; state why you believe this learning is worthwhile; and relate why this learning goal is appropriate for your students.

Content standard(s) ______________________________

Learning Goal ______________________________

Rationale ______________________________

Next Steps

The learning goals you developed for your students in Stage 1 will begin to define the learning that will take place in your classroom. Before you proceed to Stage 2: Plan, ensure that your learning goals are strong by thinking about the questions that follow:

- Why do I want to teach this?
- Why are the standards that I have chosen appropriate for my students at this time?
- How closely is my learning goal aligned with the standard(s) that I have identified?
- How relevant and meaningful to these students is what I want to teach?
- How does this learning goal connect and compare with other learning goals I have identified?

If necessary, strengthen your learning goal before you continue.[5]

Thinking about *Take One!*

Use the work you did in Stage 1 as the raw material for completing the following Composing My Written Commentary sections of your portfolio entry:

- Bulleted items that refer to Instructional Context
- Bulleted items that address your knowledge of your students

Stage 2

Plan

What is Coherent Instruction?

To be effective, instruction must be "coherent"—that is, all of the elements of instruction must relate to one another logically and purposefully. Instruction is coherent when:

- **Learning goals** are selected and learning activities and assessments are planned with students' diverse needs, abilities, interests, and cultural backgrounds in mind.
- **Learning activities and assessments** all relate strongly to learning goals and standards, and generate purposeful evidence that informs current and future instruction.
- **Instructional materials and resources** are engaging, assist students in attaining learning goals, and reflect the contributions of women and men from diverse cultures.
- **Students** are grouped according to the purposes of their learning activities and can choose learning pathways based on their needs, abilities, interests, and cultural backgrounds.
- **Lessons and units** are structured to build understanding in steps and ultimately illuminate overarching concepts.

Coherence helps students achieve deep understanding and encourages them to apply their new knowledge and skills in a relevant manner.

The graphic that follows *(Figure 4)* outlines considerations that can help you plan coherent instruction. Notice that learning goals are at the heart of the graphic, and all other elements radiate out from these goals.

The key to coherence is ensuring that the learning goals you select, as well as your knowledge of your particular students, drive all aspects of instruction. It is this close alignment of all aspects of the lesson with your learning goal and content standard(s) that makes instruction coherent.[1]

NBPTS Core Proposition 2:

Teachers know the subjects they teach and how to teach those subjects to students.

Coherence helps students achieve deep understanding and encourages them to apply their new knowledge and skills in a relevant manner.

The key to coherence is ensuring that the learning goals you select, as well as your knowledge of your particular students, drive all aspects of instruction.

The Process of Designing Coherent Instruction

1

Learning Activities

With your learning goal and knowledge of your students in mind, the first step is selecting or designing learning activities that:

- help students understand the "big ideas" of the content and achieve the learning goal
- employ processes that are appropriate to the content
- deeply engage students in learning new content and skills
- challenge students intellectually
- allow students to make choices about their learning
- provide meaningful formative assessment opportunities that allow you to monitor student learning and correct developing misunderstandings, provide feedback to students, and adjust your instruction as needed
- encourage students to make connections with previous learning as well as with their personal experiences
- present meaningful summative assessment opportunities that allow you to evaluate student learning and provide a basis for future instruction

2

Instructional Materials and Resources

With your learning goal, knowledge of your students, and learning activities in mind, the next step is choosing instructional materials and resources that:

- help students understand key concepts
- challenge students intellectually
- invite students to engage in meaningful ways with the "big ideas" of the content
- provide opportunities for students to make choices about their learning
- reflect your students' individual interests, as well as their varied learning approaches
- represent the contributions of women and men as well as those from diverse cultures, whenever feasible
- allow family members and individuals from the community to share their skills and expertise with students
- encourage students to locate some materials and resources independently

Figure 4

3

Instructional Groups

With your learning goal, knowledge of your students, and learning activities in mind, the next step is choosing ways to group students that:

- are appropriate for the particular learning activity
- assist students in understanding key concepts and allow them to learn from one another
- encourage students to engage with each other over the "big ideas" of the content
- invite students to apply their individual learning styles
- engage all students in challenging and authentic work
- expose students to viewpoints other than their own
- provide opportunities for students to share leadership, resolve conflicts, and participate in democratic processes

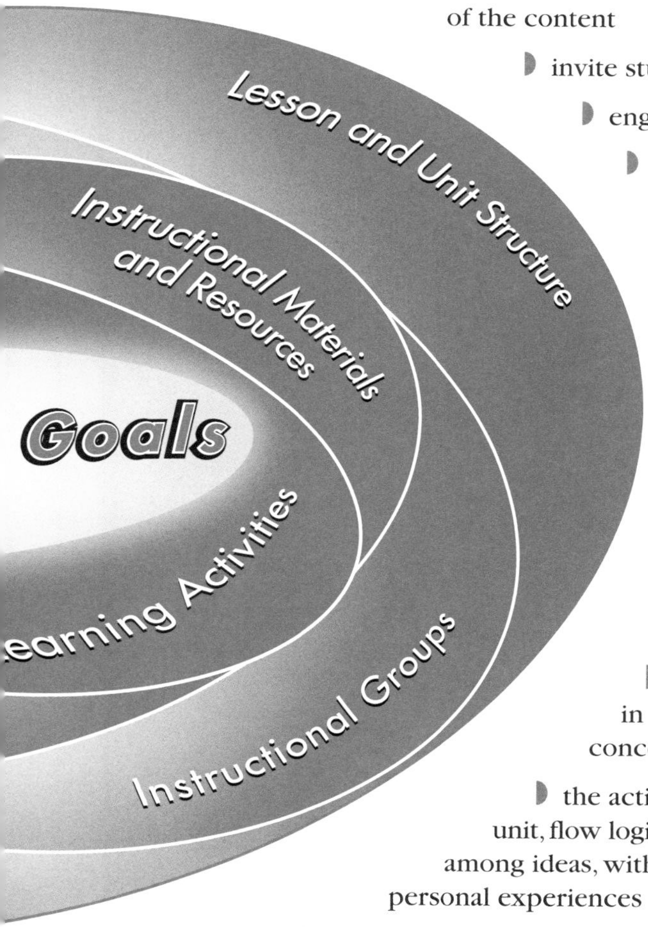

Lesson and Unit Structure

Instructional Materials and Resources

Goals

Learning Activities

Instructional Groups

4

Lesson Structure

With your learning goals and knowledge of your students in mind, the final step is structuring your lesson (and if applicable, lessons within the unit) so that:

- the sequence of learning activities scaffolds and promotes student attainment of the learning goal in steps
- each activity plays an important, sequential role in helping students thoroughly understand important concepts and improve related skills
- the activities in the lesson, and the lessons in the unit, flow logically, enabling students to make connections among ideas, with their prior learning, and with their personal experiences
- students have time to deeply explore material
- students have time to thoughtfully complete their assignments and assessments
- the planned pace of the lesson respects your students' needs and abilities, without either frustrating or boring them

Learning Activities[2]

The first element to consider when planning coherent instruction is learning activities—the structures through which teachers teach and students learn. When choosing learning activities, it is critical to consider whether and how they can help you teach the specific learning proposed in your learning goals. Will the products and demonstrations they elicit from students generate the type and amount of evidence you need to be certain your students have achieved the intended learning?

In addition, the learning activities you select must be appropriate for your particular students in terms of their prior learning, learning needs, cultural backgrounds, individual abilities, learning approaches, interests, and personal experiences.

Consult the NBPTS Standards for your discipline and developmental level to learn more about the kinds of learning activities that are most conducive to helping your students learn. Because a single kind of activity can suit neither all kinds of learning nor all students, the standards promote the use of a variety of learning activities that together:

- offer varied entry points into the curriculum, based on students' individual differences
- provide students with multiple perspectives on key matters of interest, and allow students to explore issues across the curriculum from a variety of points of view
- allow students to construct understanding from their learning experiences and connect what they learn in class to their prior learning as well as to their everyday experiences
- teach students to recognize problems, reason incisively, ask relevant questions, and develop discipline-specific attitudes and habits of mind
- invite students to share their ideas through student-to-student interaction and discussion
- give students open-ended opportunities to address significant problems and also acquaint them with techniques others have used to confront and solve important problems
- employ a rich array of instructional media, including available technologies when appropriate
- enable students with exceptional needs and abilities to participate fully in the life of the class
- provide students with varied, meaningful, regular assessment opportunities that allow them to express their understanding and that accommodate students with special learning needs
- engage students in self and peer assessment, and the creation and use of rubrics and portfolios

Employing a variety of teacher- and student-led learning activities to educate your students helps create a classroom climate of high expectations, respect, common goals, and mutual support among students.

Stop & Write About Your Practice Now

Directions: The chart entitled ***"Learning Activities A to Z"*** which follows, lists some activities that are commonly used to assist students in learning content. Complete the chart as follows:

1. As you scan the list for the first time, mark those activities you use *frequently* with an asterisk (*) and those that are new to you with a question mark (?). (Add learning activities you use but are not included at the bottom of the chart.) The activities featured on the chart are briefly defined in "Appendix B: Learning Activities." You can also consult with a colleague to learn about activities that are new to you. Stop and complete the first part of the chart now.

2. Revisit the activities you marked with an asterisk. Who does the work in the activities you use frequently? For example, in a lecture, the teacher does the work, while in a true cooperative learning activity, students do the work. Are the activities you use frequently really "minds-on"? Or are they tasks that can be completed with minimal intellectual involvement? For each activity you marked with an asterisk, make the appropriate mark in the "Engaging for Students" column:

+ highly engaging for students	– minimally engaging for students
√ somewhat engaging for students	x not at all engaging for students

3. Now look at the activities you use frequently in terms of how relevant and meaningful they are to your students. Which activities engage students in meaningful exploration of topics? Which invite students to apply skills and concepts to their own lives, backgrounds, and experiences? For each activity you marked with an asterisk, make the appropriate mark in the "Relevant and Meaningful for Students" column:

+ profoundly relevant and meaningful	– minimally relevant and meaningful
√ somewhat relevant and meaningful	x not at all relevant and meaningful

4. Finally, look at the activities you use frequently in terms of how closely they align with the NBPTS Standards for your discipline and developmental level. Which of these activities engage students in learning in ways that are promoted by the NBPTS Standards and by your academic standards? Which provide practice with key processes addressed in the standards? For each activity you marked with an asterisk, make the appropriate mark in the "Connection to Standards for Teaching" column:

+ profoundly relevant to standards	– minimally relevant to standards
√ somewhat relevant to standards	x not at all relevant to standards

5. As a follow-up, compare the range of learning activities you use in your classroom with the range of activities advocated by the NBPTS Standards. Then, choose a few activities that are new to you, learn more about them, and begin using them with your students.

Learning Activities A to Z*

Learning Activity	Frequently Used (*)	New (?)	Engaging for Students	Relevant and Meaningful for Students	Connection to Standards for Teaching
Analogies and metaphors					
Carousel brainstorm					
Case study					
Concept web					
Concept attainment					
Concept formation					
Cooperative learning					
Debate					
Demonstration					
Direct instruction					
Discussion					
Field trips					
Guest speakers					
Inquiry or experiment					
Jigsaw					
K-W-L-Q					
Learning log (journaling)					
Lecture or presentation					
Matrix (cross-classification chart)					
Mind map					
Note-taking					
Performance—dramatic					
Prediction					
Project—dramatic					
Questioning					
ReQuest					
Role-play or simulation					
SQ3R					
Stories or storytelling					
T-chart					
Think-pair-share					
Venn diagram					
Video clip					
Worksheet					
Other: _______________					
Other: _______________					

** Appendix B provides brief descriptions of these learning activities.*

Collaborative Learning Activities

Collaborative activities can make learning more interesting, meaningful, and memorable for students. In addition, these activities can encourage students to share leadership roles, teach them how to work together with different types of people, and show students that their diversity enriches their products and performances.

Successful facilitation of collaborative learning activities requires careful planning and preparation. For example, because the composition of student groups can impact how and what students learn, it's important to think about how you will group students. In addition, it is important that your students understand your expectations for team behavior. By helping students establish a "collaborative code," you can introduce them to the benefits of group work as well as the behaviors and attitudes that make it possible for each of them to reap those benefits.

What's more, before pursuing any new strategy with students, it's essential to discuss your planned approach with them so that they know what to expect. If your students are new to group work, it may also be helpful to lead them in team-building activities and to introduce them to collaboration gradually.[3]

When first faced with the prospect of working in groups, some students may fear "failing" at your approach or may feel anxious about working with peers they do not know. Leading students in activities that do not threaten their grades and that expose them gradually to increasingly challenging collaborative tasks can strengthen their confidence, quell their fears, and leave them excited about group learning.[4]

Learn More About Collaborative Learning

Depending on the NBPTS certificate area that you have selected for completing your *Take One!* portfolio entry, collaborative learning may or may not play a role in the lesson you are planning for *Take One!*. If it does, consult *"Appendix C: Collaborative Learning."*

Appendix C provides additional information about:

- assigning students to groups
- establishing a collaborative code with students
- helping students manage group work

It's Your Turn

Directions: Now that you have identified the students and learning goal that will provide the focus of your portfolio entry, and have also considered the elements of coherent instruction, the next step is to plan your lesson—that is, to select the learning activities, instructional materials and resources, student groupings, and lesson structure that are most likely to help your students achieve that learning goal.

1. Understanding the nature of the evidence that will convince you that your students have achieved the intended learning can help you select learning activities, instructional materials and resources, instructional groups, and a lesson structure that carry out the aims of your learning goal. Take a moment to think about the specific evidence that will convince you that the students you identified earlier have achieved the learning goal you specified in Stage 1. The following overarching questions can guide your thinking. Ask yourself:
   - How do I want my students to be different after I teach the lesson? What do I want them to know, understand, and be able to do as a result of instruction?
   - What would be convincing evidence that my students have gained the knowledge, skills, and abilities identified in my learning goal and content standard?
   - What would my students have to do to demonstrate that they have attained the knowledge, skills, and abilities I identified? How will I know my students have achieved the intended learning?
2. Use the questions provided below and on the next three pages for each element of instruction to help you plan the lesson that will be the focus of your *Take One!* submission.[5]

Learning Activities

With your learning goal, knowledge of your students, and the evidence you require in mind, describe the learning activities that will help the students you identified earlier achieve the learning goal you selected in Stage 1. While planning, ask yourself:

- What kinds of learning activities, tasks, or experiences can produce the types and amount of convincing evidence that I need?
- Which processes and activities are most appropriate for teaching the "big ideas" of this content, as well as related skills?
- Which activities are most appropriate for my students, given their needs, abilities, prior learning, interests, learning approaches, personal experiences, and cultural backgrounds?

- Which activities are likely to challenge and engage my students? How do I know?

Instructional Materials and Resources

With your learning goal, knowledge of your students, and learning activities in mind, list the instructional materials and resources that you will use to support your students' learning. While planning, ask yourself:

- Which instructional materials and resources are most likely to help my students understand key concepts, connect with prior learning, and reach the learning goal?
- Which will engage my students in meaningful dialogue with the "big ideas" of the content?
- Which are my students likely to find challenging, interesting, and personally relevant?
- Which show respect for my students' gender, cultural diversity, and learning styles?
- How can I involve my students in selecting meaningful materials and resources?
- How could the community or my students' families contribute to this learning?

Instructional Groups

With your learning goal, knowledge of your students, and learning activities in mind, describe how you will group students for each activity. While planning, ask yourself:

- What groupings are most appropriate for the particular learning activities I have planned?
- What groupings will help my students understand the material, engage with each other over the "big ideas" of the content, and achieve the learning goal?
- How do these groupings invite students to apply their individual learning styles?
- How will I make sure that all students participate in challenging and authentic work while grouped?
- How do these groupings encourage my students to exchange ideas, share leadership, resolve conflicts, and participate in democratic processes?

____

____

____

____

____

____

____

Lesson Structure

With your learning goal, knowledge of your students, and learning activities in mind, describe how you will structure your lesson. While planning, ask yourself:

- What role does each activity play in helping students thoroughly understand important concepts and improve related skills?
- How can I sequence these learning activities and instruction so the lesson makes sense to my students and scaffolds their learning?
- Am I sure the activities in the lesson flow logically and will enable my students to make connections among ideas, with their prior learning, and with their personal experiences?
- At what points will I assess and gather evidence of students' ongoing and cumulative learning? How will I use feedback to students to further learning?
- How much time will students need to explore material deeply and complete their assignments and assessments thoughtfully?

- What do I know about individual students' needs and abilities that can help me pace this lesson appropriately?

Next Steps

Once you are satisfied that your evidence-centered lesson plan is coherent and likely to engage all of your students in learning, it's almost time to try it out. Before you do, however, it is important to consider the impact that your classroom environment can have on student learning.

The way you structure your classroom, the spirit of learning that prevails in your classroom, and your interpersonal skills can maximize the effectiveness of your lesson or hinder its success.

Stage 3 examines specific aspects of classroom environment that encourage students to participate fully in their learning.

Thinking about *Take One!*

Use the work you did in Stage 2 as the raw material for completing the following Composing My Written Commentary sections of your portfolio entry:

- Bulleted items that refer to Instructional Planning
- Bulleted items that refer to Instructional Design
- Bulleted items that refer to Assessment of Students

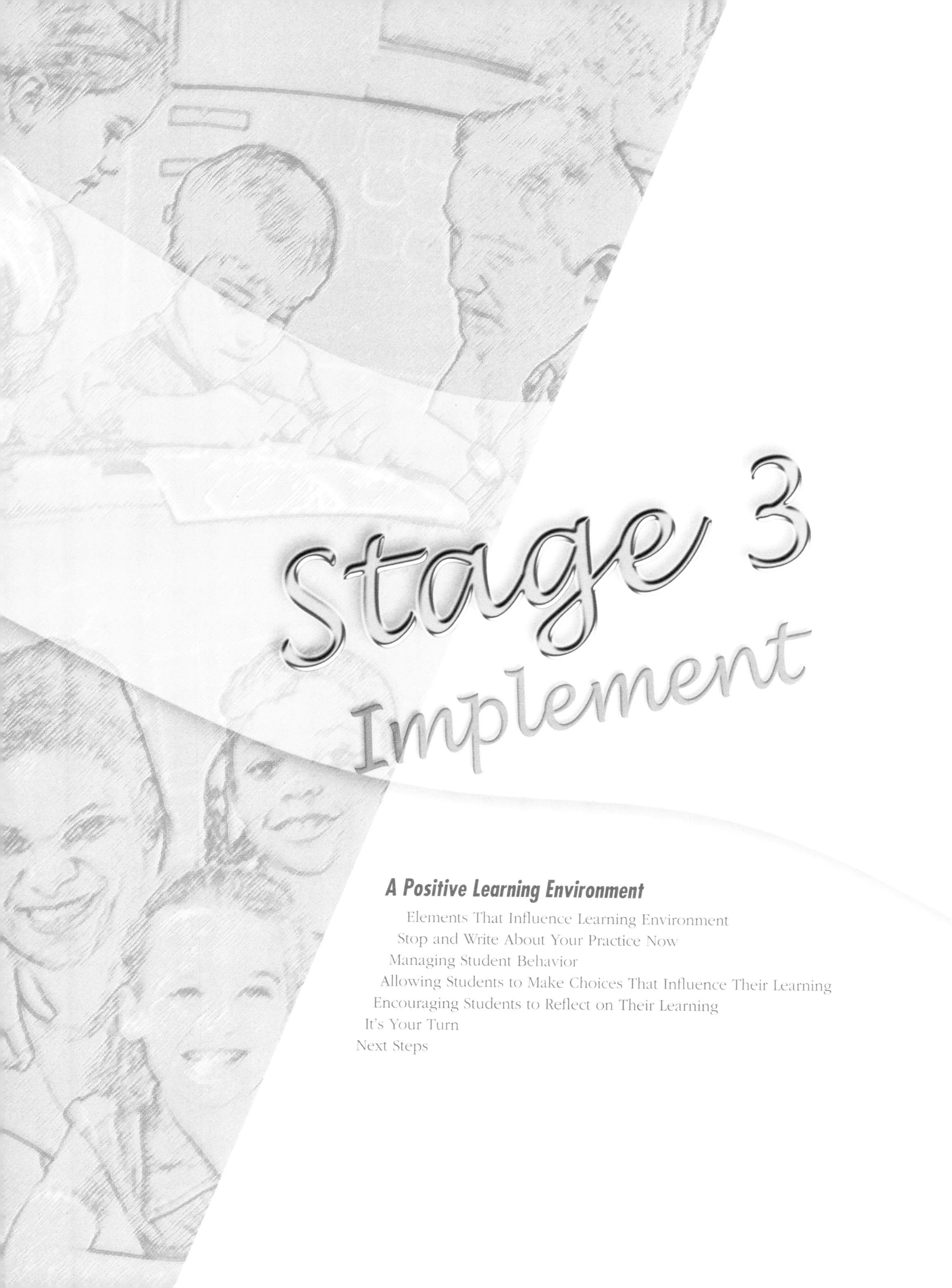

Stage 3
Implement

A Positive Learning Environment

A Positive Learning Environment

Accomplished teachers know that students must be supported if they are to take creative risks, offer conjectures, question the assertions proposed by others, or find their ideas challenged or validated. They create an atmosphere that encourages respect for diversity of culture, language, background, physical and mental condition, and experience, as well as an assumption of mutual responsibility for the success of the learning community.

In addition, accomplished teachers sensitively apply principles of fairness, particularly when grouping students; recognizing competence, effort, or performance; providing students with learning and performance options; and allocating time, learning opportunities, or other resources.

The supportive, congenial, and purposeful learning environment established by such teachers promotes active learning, exposes students to a variety of intellectual challenges, and prepares them for independent learning opportunities.[1]

Elements That Influence Learning Environment

A number of elements influence the quality of your classroom's learning environment; however, the appropriateness of each depends on your students' ages and developmental levels. In general, a climate that encourages students to participate fully in their learning arises when:

- **Teacher-student and student-student relationships are grounded in mutual respect.**
  All students feel valued and safe and know they will be treated with dignity, even when they take intellectual risks.
- **The teacher has high expectations for all students, as well as himself/herself, and students are committed to high-quality work.**
  The atmosphere is cognitively busy, with a shared sense of excitement about both the importance of learning and the significance of content.
- **The teacher and students effectively employ routines and procedures that result in the smooth operation of the classroom, maximizing time for instruction.**
  Procedures govern use of time, movement, and management of student groups as well as transitions; distribution of materials and noninstructional responsibilities; and supervision of volunteers and paraprofessionals.

NBPTS Core Proposition 3:

Teachers are responsible for managing and monitoring student learning.

- **The teacher uses agreed-upon standards of conduct, as well as clear consequences for overstepping bounds, to manage student behavior.**
  These well-run classrooms are characterized by clear and reasonable expectations for age-appropriate behavior, fairness, a high level of teacher-awareness, teacher and student self-control, and a focus on correcting student behavior, when necessary, rather than criticizing students' worth.

- **The physical environment is safe, flexible, and conducive to learning.**
  All students, including those with special needs, have access to the board, the teacher, and other learning resources. The teacher is adept at using teaching aids, such as chalkboards, flip charts, overhead projectors, VCRs, and computers, and students show ownership of their physical space.[2]

When you complete your *Take One!* portfolio entry, you will be asked to show evidence of the quality of your classroom environment. So before you move from planning your evidence-centered lesson to implementing and video recording it, focus for a moment on the learning environment and teaching skills that are likely to invite students to participate fully in the instruction you have prepared.

Stop & Write About Your Practice Now

1. Describe how you establish and maintain an atmosphere of trust, openness, and mutual respect in your classroom (e.g., model respectful language, recognize students who demonstrate respect).

____

____

____

____

____

____

2. Describe how you encourage students to take responsibility for their own learning and to take pride in their work (e.g., offer choice in activities, teach students to pace themselves on a big project, employ self-assessment skills).

____

____

____

____

____

____

3. Describe how you convey the importance of the content and your expectations for achievement (e.g., connect content to real-life applications, require revision of work that does not meet quality standards).

____

____

____

____

____

____

(continued on next page)

4. Describe how you make your physical environment conducive to optimal student learning (e.g., chairs in a circle for a discussion, desks pushed into "tables" for science activities, students with visual impairments in the front).

____

____

____

____

____

____

5. Discuss the classroom routines and procedures that you employ (e.g., distribution and collection of materials, transitions between activities), including how you establish and implement them.

____

____

____

____

____

____

6. Describe how you establish standards of conduct and respond to behavior that does not meet school or classroom guidelines (e.g., establishing and posting classroom expectations, conducting classroom meetings, assigning direction).

____

____

____

____

____

____

____

Managing Student Behavior

Successful managers of student behavior use an array of teaching strategies and skills to influence student behavior and achieve order before misbehavior has an opportunity to occur.

Order generally occurs when:

- **students are aware** of the teachers' expectations, procedures, and consequences for misbehavior
- the **classroom and learning activities are well organized** and transitions flow smoothly
- the **teacher has high expectations** for students' intellectual achievements
- **students understand** what it means to behave appropriately
- **students are engaged** in challenging, meaningful work
- students and teachers **treat one another with respect**
- the **teacher is aware** of what students are doing at all times
- students and teachers have **confidence in the classroom environment**
- the physical **environment is conducive to learning**

Teachers' individual approaches to managing student behavior often reflect their own styles and personalities, as well as the personalities and developmental needs of their students. However, becoming a skilled manager of student behavior does not *depend* on your personality. It is a learned skill.

The establishment of order is an ongoing process that usually begins in September when students are presented with, or enlisted in developing, general rules of behavior. These norms help students learn classroom procedures and communicate what is expected of them both behaviorally and academically.

Once a code of behavior is in place, it is reinforced throughout the year. As the school year proceeds, the teacher consistently and impartially enforces the code of behavior in the classroom. A key to student respect for the rules is the knowledge that the same code applies to all students.

At the same time, your efforts to manage your classroom may be in vain if students do not have an opportunity to engage in work that interests and challenges them. A well-managed classroom that does not provide a mental

Pause and Reflect

What are your behavior-management strengths? In which aspects of behavior management would you most like to improve?

challenge may leave students searching for an outlet for their ingenuity. It may not be long before all of their cleverness is misdirected in the form of ingenious—as well as not so ingenious—misbehavior.[4]

Allowing Students to Make Choices That Influence Their Learning

One way in which you can increase your students' engagement is by allowing them to make important choices about their learning. As with other aspects of their learning, your students will need your support to make these decisions wisely.

Generally, the complexity and number of choices you ask students to make about their learning should grow with their age and skill level. When learning new skills, students may appreciate being asked to make a few choices. After they develop some facility with skill, they can also make more important decisions. With each new level of choice, you present opportunities for students to learn decision-making skills side-by-side with their content learning.

The most important choices students can make about their learning involve what they should learn and how they should learn it. Allowing students to choose the content that will achieve your learning goals—and allowing them to influence how they will arrive at that learning—are powerful engagement tools.

One way to help students make wise choices about their learning is to share with them the curriculum standards or instructional goals you are responsible for teaching. For example, math standards in your district may direct students to "collect, organize, describe, represent, and interpret data." After sharing the standards, you might tell students, "You need to show me that you can graph and analyze data. I would like you to choose both the data you will use and what you will seek to determine from that data."

To help students along, you could provide a template for their decision-making, such as "I will collect information about _____ and I will determine _____." In response, a student may decide, "I will collect information about rainfall in Florida, Maine, Washington, and Arizona, and I will determine the average rainfalls per year." Or, "I will collect information about movie sales, and I will determine what types of movies sell the most tickets." You may also want to ask students to specify the kinds of graphs they will use, and depending on their ages, you could ask for deeper analysis.[5]

Pause and Reflect

What kinds of choices do students make in your classroom? In which areas could they be making more meaningful choices?

Encouraging Students to Reflect on Their Learning

Regular opportunities to reflect on their learning can help make students more aware of the unique ways in which they learn. One goal of this kind of reflection is to help students make informed choices about their learning. For example, asking students to reflect on the types of learning experiences that most excite them can help them incorporate such elements into their decisions about how to pursue particular content. Similarly, heightened awareness of their individual thinking and learning processes can help students choose methods of demonstrating their learning that make the best use of their skills and abilities.

Journal writing and discussion directed by focused questions are two effective methods for eliciting this type of reflection from students. For example, after students complete an active learning experience, it may be useful to allow them to discuss a few of the following questions in groups, or to provide them with an opportunity to reflect more personally in their journals. (It may help to remind students to be specific and provide examples.)

Journal writing and discussion directed by focused questions are two effective methods for eliciting this type of reflection from students.

- "What did I find most interesting about this learning experience?"
- "What did I find most challenging?"
- "What did I do best on this assignment?"
- "What (and how) could I have done better?"
- "What did I learn about ______?"
- "What did I learn about myself?"
- "What would I like to do again?"

In addition to asking students to reflect on their academic work, it can also be helpful to provide opportunities for students to reflect on their group-process skills and their learning styles. You can also accomplish this by posing questions:

- "What did we do best together when working on this project?"
- "What (and how) could we work better as a team?"
- "How did working in groups help me learn?"
- "How did I apply my learning styles during this project?"
- "At what point in this learning experience did I come to understand the new information?"
- "What did I do with the information that helped me to understand it? Did I read it, write about it, talk about it, or something else?"
- "Which way of working with the information did I like best?"[6]

Pause and Reflect

In what ways do you invite your students to reflect on themselves as learners? How could you provide more meaningful reflection opportunities?

It's Your Turn

Video Recording Your Lesson

Take One! requires that you submit a video of your teaching to support your analysis and evaluation of your proficiency; your video should show the National Board assessors how you interact with students, the climate you create in the classroom, and the ways in which you engage your students in learning.

Capturing the many different aspects of the classroom for others to observe sometimes presents challenges for teachers, so useful tips for video recording your lesson are included with your *Take One!* materials. Be sure to read these materials closely for information about the required length and format of your video, using video equipment, and practicing teaching in front of a video camera (see the directions for your entry as well as "Video Recording Overview" on your CD-ROM).

It may take a while before you and your students feel comfortable with this process.[7]

Implementing Your Lesson

When you are comfortable with the video recording process, implement and tape your planned lesson. As you teach, keep these questions in mind:

- In what ways are my students progressing toward the learning goals? What do they grasp? How are their skills developing? Is the pace of the lesson appropriate?

- Which aspects of the content and skills at the heart of this lesson do they find challenging? Where are they having difficulty making connections? Who needs additional help and how can I provide it?
- Are my students engaged? Who is losing interest and why? Are they grouped effectively? How can I help all of my students persist through their learning activities and assessment tasks?

Don't be afraid to make purposeful adjustments as you teach; your flexibility and sensitivity to your students' needs may make the difference in how deeply they learn.[8]

Next Steps

An essential part of the implementation of your lesson is the collection of evidence. While your video is a significant piece of evidence, samples of student work, your anecdotal observations, and other evidence are also critical. In Stage 4, these artifacts provide the basis for your interpretation and analysis of the lesson. The more varied and abundant your evidence is, the more valid your conclusions can be.

It is also important to remember that there is no such thing as a "perfect" video of a classroom activity. In fact, assessors are trained to expect to see signs of real-world classrooms—such as the interruption of a bell or intercom or the student who is not completely on task. What is important is your articulation of your practice, your awareness of the interaction among your students, your learning goals, and your instruction.

Thinking about *Take One!*

Use the work you did in Stage 3 as the raw material for completing the following Composing My Written Commentary sections of your portfolio entry:

- Bulleted items that address establishing a classroom environment
- Bulleted items that address fairness, equity, and access for all students

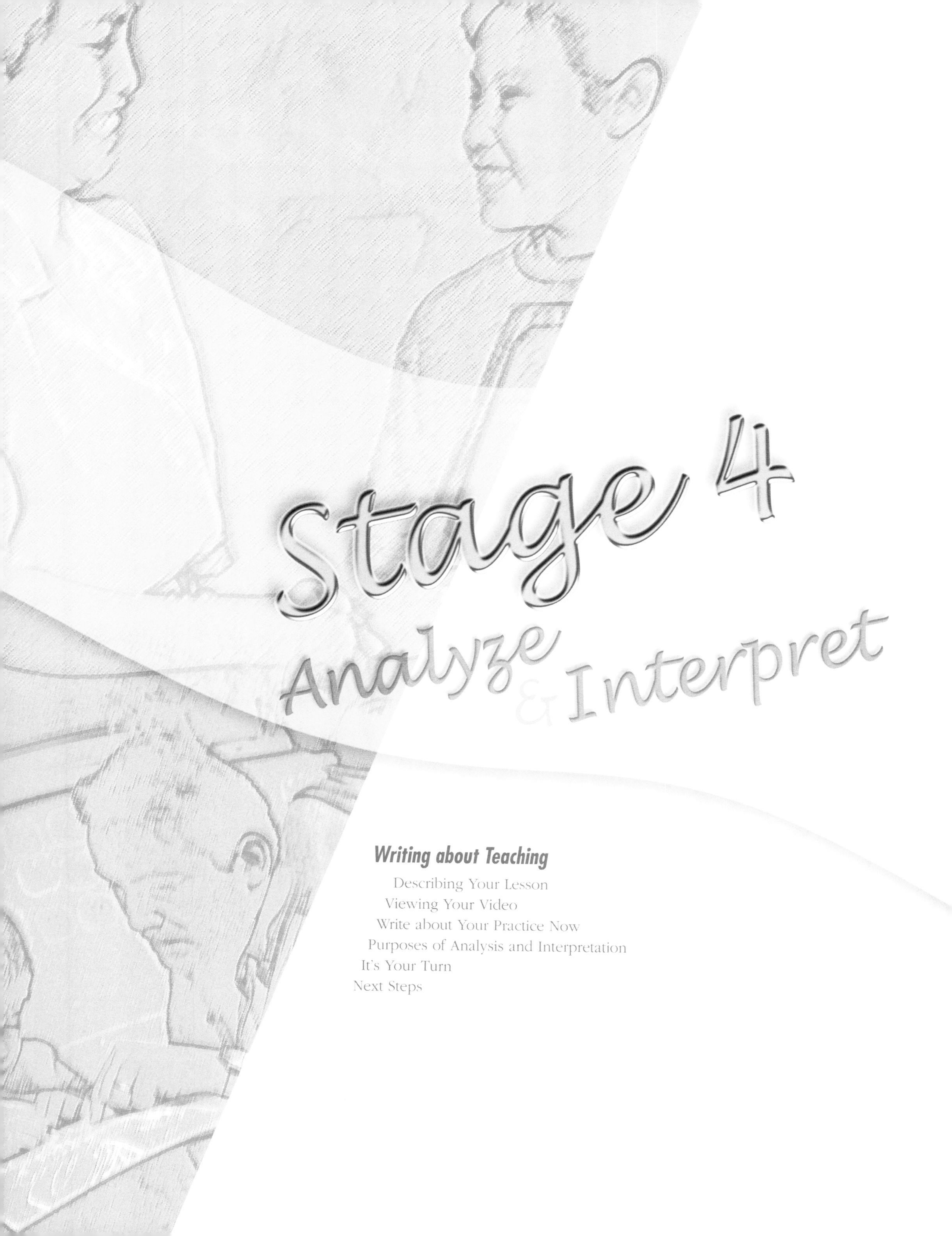

Stage 4
Analyze & Interpret

Writing about Teaching

Writing about Teaching

Now that you have had an opportunity to implement a planned, evidence-centered lesson, the next step is analyzing and interpreting the evidence you collected in order to determine the impact the lesson had on your students' learning, as well as on your teaching proficiency.

This involves three steps. First, you will review and describe the evidence. Next, you will ask questions about the evidence and think analytically about what took place and why. In doing so, you will arrive at the third step, your interpretation of what took place. Later, in Stage 5, you will add two additional steps: You will reflect on the success of your efforts and consider ways to apply your learning to future teaching.

In completing your portfolio entry, it's important that you keep all of these thinking tasks separate in your mind. You will be asked to provide insight into not just "what is happening" in your classroom (description), but the rationale for those events and processes (interpretation), and eventually, what you learned about yourself professionally (reflection) that can help you teach more effectively (application).

> **NBPTS Core Proposition 4:**
>
> *Teachers think systematically about their practice and learn from experience.*

Because it is not always a part of the daily practice of teaching, some teachers may have little practice in such description, analysis, and reflection. What's more, thinking analytically about teaching is complicated because teaching is complicated. Thus, it may be helpful to gain some practice with this kind of thinking and writing before completing your portfolio entry.

Describe

Consider a completed assignment that elicited substantial information about your students' understandings. Examine one student sample. As you do, ask yourself: What did this student do correctly or incorrectly? What are the most striking features of this student's response? (Use additional paper, if needed, for your response.)

Analyze and Interpret

Continuing with the same sample, ask yourself, "What do the features I noted tell me about this learner?" How does the response fit with what I already know about this student's understandings and performance? What does it tell me that I may not have realized before? What did this student learn, and in what ways does this student need to improve? (Use additional paper, if needed, for your response.)

Remember, regardless of the strength of the evidence that you present in your portfolio entry, a crucial element in your Written Commentary is your analysis and interpretation of what happened in your featured lesson. Through this commentary you must demonstrate to assessors that you understood what took place and used what you learned appropriately in your teaching.[1]

Before proceeding with Stage 4, review the "Get Started" section of your CD-ROM—particularly the subsection entitled "Writing about Teaching." This information can help you respond more appropriately to questions. You may also benefit from the subsection called "Analysis Practice." Together, the writing examples and suggestions provided in these sections can help you present a clearer picture of your practice to assessors.

In addition to support materials provided with *Take One!*, your responses to the questions in this activity book can help you dig beneath the surface of the daily details of your teaching. Systematic and probing questions that ask "why," "how," and "so what" are key to analyzing your practice and beginning to reflect on it. Depending on your readiness for the assessment, you may be able to use your responses to these prewriting activities as the basis for your Written Commentary.

Describing Your Lesson

Before you begin analyzing how well your students achieved the learning goal you set, you must understand what happened during your lesson. As ***the following chart*** shows, when writing about teaching, different language is used to distinguish the *what* (the description) from the *why* (analysis and interpretation). The activities that follow are intended to help you zoom in on what transpired during your evidence-centered lesson so that you can describe it for assessors.

You will be asked to provide insight into not just "what is happening" in your classroom (description), but the rationale for those events and processes (interpretation), and eventually, what you learned about yourself professionally (reflection) that can help you teach more effectively (application).

Words You Can Use to Introduce

Description	Interpretation
uses	understands
displays	knows
makes	is aware of
shows	demonstrates
does	can apply
says	remembers
repeats	needs help with
lists	comprehends
provides	appears to have
identifies	able to
writes	exhibits
presents	little evidence of
utilizes	shows evidence of
omits	maintains
includes	consistently
completes	is inconsistent
misses	develops
ignores	organizes

Adapted/reprinted with permission from *Understanding Early Literacy Learning Facilitator's Kit*. Princeton, NJ, ETS, 2003. Available: http://www.ets.org/pathwise.

Viewing Your Video

Before attempting to respond to the questions in Stage 4, watch the video with a focus on the implementation of your lesson plan. (See "Video Recording Overview" in the "Get Started" section of your *Take One!* CD-ROM.)

If you are not accustomed to seeing yourself on video, you may be tempted to be concerned with your appearance or with overused words, like "uh." While these observations can be helpful, try to keep your focus on the lesson—the teaching and learning.

Watch the video more than once so you can concentrate more effectively. In addition, you may choose to watch the video with a colleague; this "second pair of eyes" may notice aspects of the lesson you didn't see, and may also be able to provide you with helpful feedback.[2]

Write about Your Practice Now[3]

As you view your video, compare your lesson plan with the video of the actual lesson. In the space that follows, take notes that *describe* what took place during the lesson. (Refer to the graphic on the previous page if you need to remind yourself of useful descriptive language.) Describe any omissions, additions, deviations, and modifications you made in your lesson plan, and note both positive and negative effects that these changes had on student learning. It may also be helpful to note the time each activity took, as well as steps you took to ensure fairness, equity, and access to learning for all students in your class. Look for things that help you articulate your practice.[4]

Purposes of Analysis and Interpretation

Once you feel you have absorbed *what* happened during your lesson, the next step is to think about *why*. Analyzing how carefully planning and implementing an evidence-centered lesson impacted your students' achievement of your learning goal can help you articulate why your teaching practices are effective, as well as better understand how your students learn. The activity that follows is intended to help you do this.

Interpreting

The following points are important in interpreting:

- Interpretation provides a teacher the opportunity to assign some meaning or intent to the classroom-based evidence, beyond just describing it.
- Interpretation brings the teacher back to the standards and curricular goals.
- It is through interpretation that patterns of learning can be identified for both groups and individual children.
- Interpretation provides the means for the teacher to explain the evidence and what it means to students' families.

Adapted with permission from: ETS. (2003). *Understanding Early Literacy Learning Facilitator's Kit* (Session 6, Handout 6-3). Princeton, NJ.

It's Your Turn

1. What did you learn about your teaching from watching yourself on video?

____

____

____

____

____

____

____

____

2. Cite evidence from the video that demonstrates the coherence of your instructional design.[4]

____

____

____

____

____

____

3. Cite evidence from the video that shows how well your students achieved the learning goals for the lesson. What additional evidence supports your answer?

____

____

____

____

____

____

4. How did your purposeful design and execution of this lesson affect the achievement of your learning goals? (Your explanation should include, but not be limited to, such things as your ongoing informal assessment of your students' understanding, your anticipation and handling of misconceptions, unexpected questions from students, unanticipated opportunities for learning that you captured, or your planned strategy and its outcome in the lesson.)

____

____

____

____

____

____

____

5. How do interactions captured on the video illustrate your ability to help all of your students explore and understand the ideas being studied?

6. What interactions captured on the video show students learning to reason and think, and to communicate that reasoning and thinking? (With reference to specific interactions in the video, explain why the interactions demonstrate reasoning and thinking, as well as why they demonstrate student understanding of the topic for these particular students.)[5]

7. To what degree were you successful in improving the effectiveness of your instruction through the design and implementation of this lesson? What is the evidence for your conclusions?

8. To which of your actions do you attribute the success of the lesson? (Be specific.)[6]

Next Steps

The work you completed in Stage 4 can help you to reflect on what your lesson has taught you about your teaching. In Stage 5, you will respond to questions that guide your reflection, then consider such questions as:

- How will what you discovered through this process impact your reteaching of this lesson? What did you do well? What will you do differently next time?
- How will what you learned impact your teaching in general? What did you learn about how your students learn that can help you teach any lesson more effectively?

Thinking about *Take One!*

Use the work you did in Stage 4 as the raw material for completing the following Composing My Written Commentary sections of your portfolio entry:

- Bulleted items that refer to analyzing or interpreting your video recorded lesson
- Bulleted items that refer to analyzing instruction

Stage 5

Reflect & Apply

Enhancing Instructional Decision-Making

Enhancing Instructional Decision-Making

The end-goal of evidence-centered teaching is to gather, describe, and interpret evidence of student learning in order to improve instructional decision-making and enhance the learning of all students.

After you have taken steps to get to know your learners, to develop a coherent lesson, to create an environment that is conducive to learning, and to thoughtfully evaluate the evidence generated by your evidence-centered teaching, you are ready to apply what you have learned to improve instruction.

How you decide to apply your findings depends in part on the stage at which you gathered it. Is the evidence formative? Summative? Is it a reflection of your students as learners? The questions in the subsection, "After the Lesson," can help you determine how you can use what you learned about your students—who they are as well as what they know and can do—to make the aims of evidence-centered teaching a reality.

Questions for Applying What You Have Learned

- What will you continue to do in your instruction?
- What will you add to your instruction?
- What will you do differently in your instruction to advance your students' learning?

Adapted/reprinted with permission from *Understanding Early Literacy Learning: Facilitator's Kit* (Handout 8-1). Princeton, NJ: ETS, 2003. Available: http://www.ets.org/pathwise.

NBPTS Core Proposition 5:

Teachers are members of learning communities.

The end-goal of evidence-centered teaching is to gather, describe, and interpret evidence of student learning in order to improve instructional decision-making and enhance the learning of all students.

After the Lesson

- To what degree did your learners master the content standard(s) and learning goal around which you designed this lesson? Did they perform as you expected? If not, why did particular aspects of their understanding fall short of your expectations?
- Are there aspects of the lesson—such as misunderstandings—that you should reteach? Should this remediation be targeted toward individuals, small groups, or the entire class? And if the latter, how can you involve or further challenge students who already understand the content?
- Are students ready for the next level of understanding? How will their individual levels of understanding help or hinder their future learning? What did you learn that can help you select more appropriate instructional strategies or provide greater support for these learners in the future?
- How will you assign grades? What kind of feedback will help your students improve? What opportunities will students have to self-evaluate and possibly revise their work?[1]

Stop & Write About Your Practice Now[2]

1. In general, how successful was the lesson? Did the students learn what you intended?

   Describe a successful moment/aspect of the lesson.

2. To what extent were the lesson's goals and objectives appropriate for your students?

3. To what extent were your assessment strategies effective? Would you make any changes in your approach to assessment? If so, what changes would you make, and why?

(continued on next page)

4. To what extent was your feedback to students accurate, substantive, constructive, specific, and timely? How might you have responded differently?

____

____

____

____

____

____

Describe an instance in which your feedback positively affected a student's learning.

____

____

____

____

____

____

____

5. Comment on the different aspects (learning activities, instructional materials and resources, instructional groups, lesson structure) of your instructional delivery. To what extent was each aspect effective? How could you improve each aspect?

____

____

____

____

____

____

____

____

____

(continued on next page)

6. What, if anything, did not go as planned? What do you wish you had done differently?

____

____

____

____

____

____

7. How could you handle this aspect of the lesson differently the next time you teach it?

____

____

____

____

____

____

8. How will you use what you learned to plan future instruction?

____

____

____

____

____

____

9. How will the outcome of this lesson influence your students' future learning?

____

____

____

____

____

Developing an Action Plan

In the end, some of the findings you derive from your careful evaluation of your lessons will truly reflect your impact on student learning, while others will be best explained by curricular choices, instructional methods, the content or format of a particular assessment, students' test-taking skills, and/or the unique circumstances, personalities, and cognitive profiles of individual students.

Thus, each result is likely to contribute in a different way to a classroom-level plan of action that can help you improve your students' learning—as well as to a school-level plan of action that engages all school personnel in improving existing curricula, policies, and practices.

Remember, however, that the goal of any action plan is to more effectively teach the content standards to improve student learning. Any changes you or your school implements simply to raise test scores or meet the needs of a specific test are likely in the end to undermine the very performances you wish to strengthen.

Thus, it is important to carefully examine the findings your evaluations of student performance generate; to candidly reflect on your classroom practices; and to intentionally remediate those elements of instruction that are likely to lead to deeper student understanding and to help your students become more able, flexible demonstrators of their learning.

The goal of any action plan is to more effectively teach the content standards to improve student learning.

It's Your Turn

Directions: Translate what you have learned from this lesson into an action plan for future teaching. For example, among other things, you might describe steps you will take to: develop your understanding of individual learners, implement instructional strategies that invite deeper student understanding, provide greater support for individual learners during instruction and assessment, improve your content or pedagogical content knowledge, plan more coherent evidence-centered lessons, incorporate more technology into your lessons, enhance your learning environment, or become more adept at regularly reflecting on teaching practice.[3]

____

____

____

____

____

____

____

____

____

____

Thinking about *Take One!*

Use the work you did in Stage 5 as the raw material for completing the following Composing My Written Commentary sections of your portfolio entry:

- Bulleted items that refer to Reflection

Conclusion

Are You Ready to Complete Your *Take One!* Portfolio Entry?

Are You Ready to Complete Your *Take One!* Portfolio Entry?

Your readiness for building the portfolio component of *Take One!* depends strongly on your individual level of comfort and experience with the aspects of professional practice outlined in this activity book—getting to know your students; planning coherent, evidence-centered instruction for your students; cultivating a supportive and stimulating learning environment for your students; analyzing the connections between student learning and your own teaching; and reflecting on the effectiveness of your teaching for the purpose of improving the instruction you provide.

To decide whether you are ready, take a step back and examine your responses to the activities throughout this activity book. How tightly connected are the various aspects of your planning, implementation, and analysis? Are there any "holes" or areas where connections are a weak reflection of your teaching practice or your writing? Can you make your connections stronger by rethinking and revising your commentary? If so, you may be ready to complete your *Take One!* portfolio entry.

How Will My Response Be Scored?

The National Board Standards emphasize that accomplished teachers in every field and at every developmental level are aware of what they are doing and why they are doing it. They are conscious of where they want their students' learning to go and how they want to help them get there. Further, they continuously assess their progress toward these goals and adjust their strategies and plans accordingly.

Accomplished practice also shows itself in the teacher's ability to set high and appropriate goals for student learning, to plan worthwhile learning experiences that help students reach those goals, and to articulate the connections between the goals and the experiences.

What's more, accomplished teachers analyze classroom interactions, student work products, and their own actions and plans in order to reflect on their practice and continually renew and reconstruct their goals and strategies.

When you feel that the aspects of your practice show this kind of connectedness —when, as described in the Introduction, all strands of the double helix are wrapped cohesively—we hope that *Take One!* can bring you closer to your goal of enhanced teaching practice.[1]

Four Levels of Performance

For specific information about how *Take One!* is scored for your certificate area, see "How Will My Response Be Scored?" on your CD-ROM. In general, all portfolio entries are scored based on the strength of the connections that link the components of each portfolio entry. NBPTS assessors are practicing classroom teachers who teach in the same certificate area that they are assessing and who have been thoroughly trained and have successfully qualified to serve as an assessor.

There are four levels of performance:

- **Level 4** performances provide clear, consistent, and convincing evidence of accomplished teaching.
- **Level 3** performances provide clear evidence of accomplished teaching.
- **Level 2** performances provide limited evidence of accomplished teaching.
- **Level 1** performances provide little or no evidence of accomplished teaching.

While the scoring guidelines for each certificate area also include criteria that are relevant to teaching the specific content, **in general, all portfolio entries are examined to determine whether candidates:**

- use knowledge of their students to design a range of meaningful, interesting, and personally relevant instruction that helps increase students' understanding
- enable students to have firsthand experiences and expand their awareness
- use content knowledge to make principled decisions for instruction
- select instructional approaches that are consistent with what is known about how learners acquire understanding
- provide a stimulating and supportive learning environment
- use, and adapt as needed, authentic materials to enhance student understanding
- enable students to show what they know and can do by completing real-world tasks
- continuously analyze the relationship between teaching practice and student learning, and in light of that analysis, reevaluate and rethink their instructional choices
- accurately describe their teaching, analyze it fully and thoughtfully, and reflect on its implications and significance for future practice[2]

Evaluating the Strength of Your Connections

Figure 5 provides a useful way to think about the connections that should link the components of your portfolio entry. The rectangle at the top of the diagram represents all of the events and interactions that take place in your classroom during a lesson. Those that are circled indicate the selection of "good" evidence—evidence that is clearly related to the portfolio component on which you are working. This evidence provides the basis of the interpretations and judgments you make about the lesson for your portfolio entry. When there is coherence among these elements—for instance, when it is clear that your evidence is well chosen, sufficient, consistent, convincing, and accords with your conclusions—your connections are strong.[3]

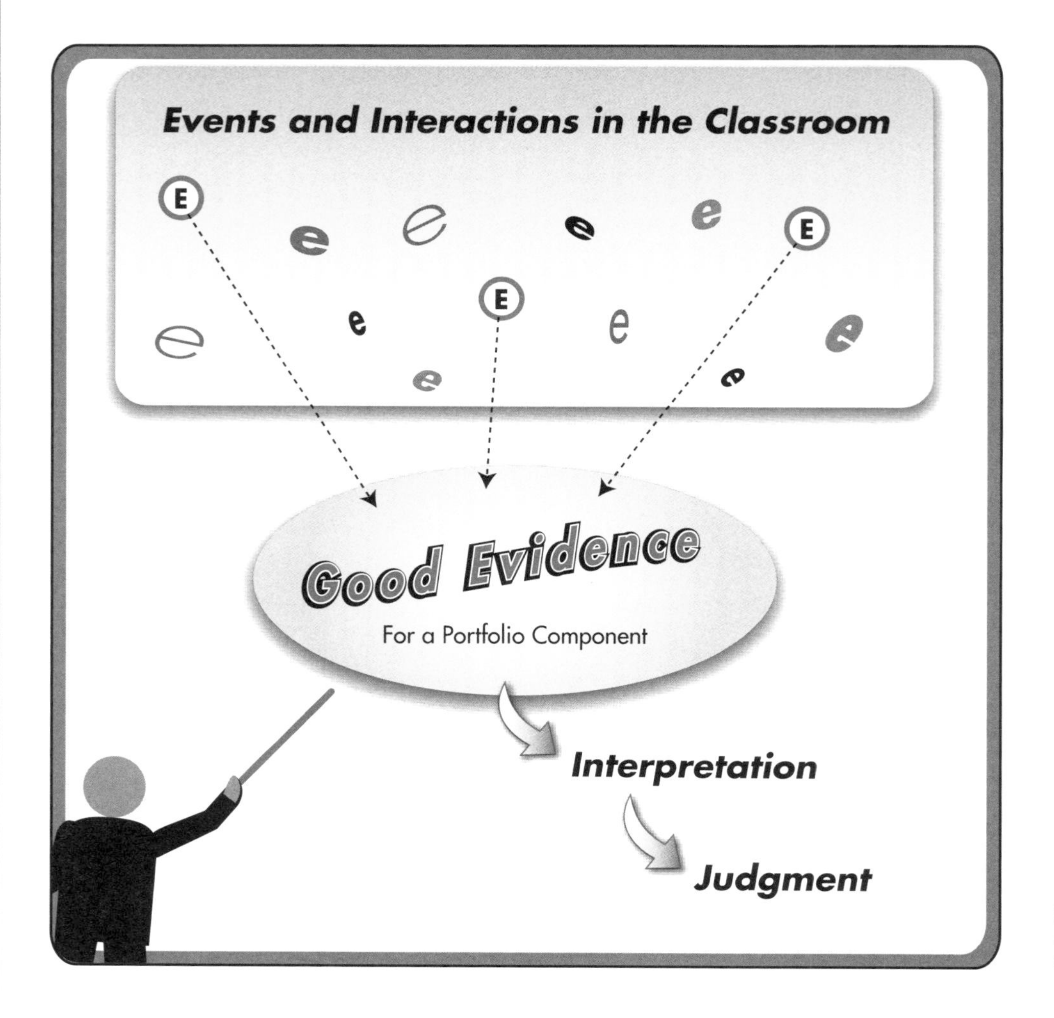

Figure 5
Making Connections

The Score Scale and the Architecture of Accomplished Teaching

As noted earlier, the Architecture of Accomplished Teaching uses a double helix to illustrate the carefully woven, upwardly spiraling nature of accomplished teaching. In this way of thinking about accomplished teaching, knowledge of students, the selection of learning goals, the planning and adapting of instruction, analysis of what works for your students, and reflection on improving future student learning are all happening at various, closely linked stages.

Figure 6 extends the metaphor by illustrating what happens to the double helix at different levels of performance. In general, at lower levels of performance, the strands that comprise the double helix are not as tight: The double helix begins to fall apart.[4]

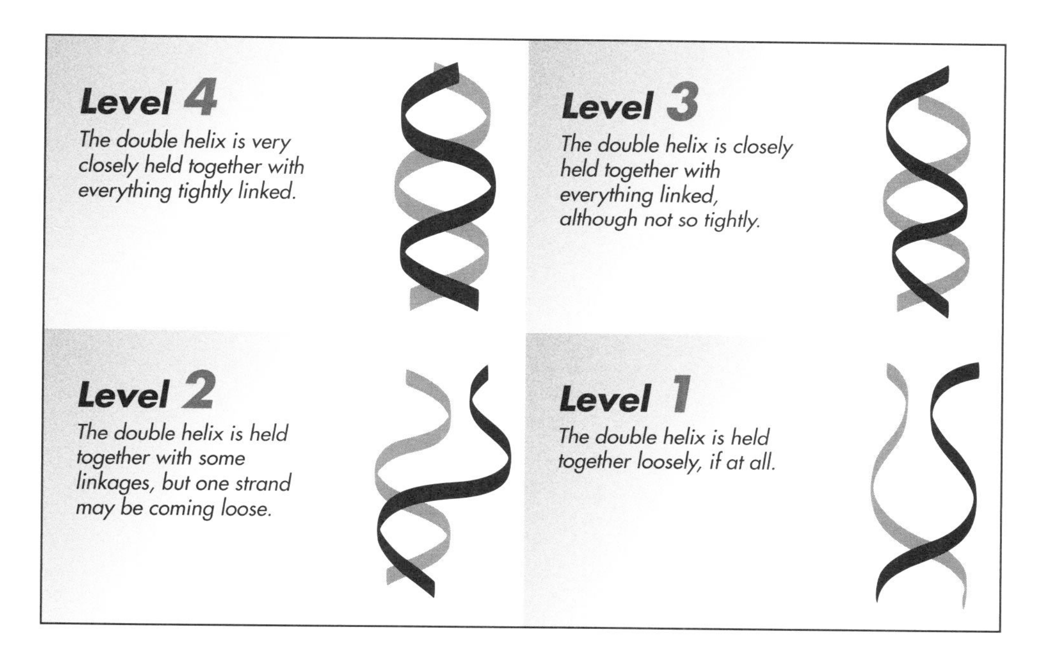

Figure 6
The Architectural Double Helix at Different Levels of Performance

Planning Your Future Advancement

Regardless of the level of success you have so far achieved in your practice, the final step before repeating the evidence-centered teaching cycle outlined in this activity book is using what you learned about your practice to begin planning the next steps of your professional development. As a result of your self-reflection, you are likely satisfied with some areas of your practice and find that there are others you wish to improve. By taking notes and outlining plans now, you can begin sketching a map to guide your future professional growth.

The action plan you developed earlier shows how you intend to use your current level of expertise to greater advantage during future instruction. But in the course of completing the activities in this activity book, you probably also discovered areas in which you would like to expand your expertise. For instance, you may want to learn more about a particular learning theory or instructional strategy. Or perhaps you would like to extend your content knowledge. How will you go about this learning?

Why not note your ideas for your professional development while they are fresh in your thoughts? In the space that follows, jot down any and all aspects of your practice that you wish to refine—whether you will attend to this learning in your next teaching cycle or later. Then, consider the scope of your plans and how you can achieve them incrementally.

Later, when you repeat the teaching cycle presented in this activity book, you can review your notes and set a new goal for your professional advancement. When that time arrives, you may follow your map exactly, or you may journey in an unanticipated direction. It matters not. Whether you see the path before you or behind you, the process of continually reflecting on and assessing your progress will pave your way to enhanced professional practice and improved student learning.[5]

My Next Steps

Appendices

Appendix A: Investigative Tools

Summary of Investigative Tools

Investigative Tool	Information About
Developmental Models: —Piaget's Stages of Childhood Development —Bruner's Theory of Children's Cognitive Development —Vygotsky's Zone of Proximal Development —Age-Group Milestone Models	• characteristics of age group • students' varied approaches to learning
Learning-Style Models: —Gardner's Multiple Intelligences —Kolb and Fry —4MAT —Dunn and Dunn	• students' varied approaches to learning
Formal observation **Informal observation**	• students' varied approaches to learning • students' skills and knowledge • students' interests and cultural heritage
Interest Inventories and Surveys	• students' interests and cultural heritage
Records: —Report cards —Records from previous schools —Standardized test scores —IEPs —Results from diagnostic testing —Reports from physicians, counselors, education consultants	• students' skills and knowledge • students' varied approaches to learning • students' interests and cultural heritage
People: —Colleagues —Guidance counselors —Administrators —Family members —Students themselves	• students' skills and knowledge • students' varied approaches to learning • students' interests and cultural heritage
Other tools: —Pre-tests and post-tests —Games —Assignments	• students' skills and knowledge • students' varied approaches to learning • students' interests and cultural heritage

To learn more these investigative tools, see: Baer, D. (2003). *Demonstrating knowledge of students.* Princeton, NJ: ETS.

Appendix B: Learning Activities

Stage 1: Learning Goal or Activity?

Following are suggested answers for *Stop and Write About Your Practice Now,* Activity A: Learning Goal or Activity?.

Note: Some of the statements in this activity that are labeled as "goals" are skeletons of high-quality goals. For the purpose of this activity, not every example has been expanded to explicitly state measurable goals (e.g., In #2, a more detailed version might read: Draw an example of an isosceles, an equilateral, and a right triangle).

When determining a goal, a teacher may want to first think through: *What will the student be able to do after this lesson? Is it measurable? How might it be measured?* Given the limited context of this activity, some of the suggested answers below may be arguable.

1. G	4. G	7. G or A	10. A	13. A
2. G	5. A	8. A	11. A	14. G
3. A	6. G	9. G	12. G	15. A

Learning Activities A to Z

Analogies and Metaphors

- **Analogy**—Students identify relationships between pairs of concepts; for example, "hot is to cold as day is to night."
- **Metaphor**—Students determine abstract or nonliteral relationships between two items; for example, "The brain is like a jungle because it is a complex system of nerves, all interconnected and dependent on each other."

Carousel Brainstorm—The carousel brainstorm is used to generate multiple ideas or solutions. Working in small groups, students rotate around the room contributing their ideas to charts and reviewing the ideas of their peers.

Case Study—Students examine real-world scenarios that feature ambiguous or multifaceted issues and work together to come to an understanding.

Concept Web—Students organize information about a topic in a graphic organizer that shows main ideas, supporting details, and their relationships.

Concept Attainment—Concept attainment is a classification activity that helps students construct an understanding of new concepts. Students are offered examples and nonexamples of a withheld "mystery concept" and asked to compare and contrast the characteristics of these until they arrive at the actual concept.

Concept Formation—Concept formation requires students to recognize and construct patterns by classifying ideas or data.

Cooperative Learning—Cooperative learning is an instructional strategy that involves students working together—either in pairs or in small clusters of three to six students—to complete meaningful academic tasks and to develop teamwork and communication skills.

Debate—Students research two or more opposing viewpoints and debate their pros and cons.

Demonstration—The teacher demonstrates a process or concept to the students; for example, using a hairdryer to blow sand when teaching the process of erosion.

Direct Instruction—The teacher leads the students in mastery of basic skills through a carefully paced, sequential teacher-directed lesson. The teacher states the objective, models the skill, asks students to copy the model, and provides feedback on the students' use of the new skill as well as time for guided practice.

Discussion—The teacher opens up a topic for discussion, encouraging and appreciating varied opinions and ideas offered by the students.

Field Trip—Students experience the curriculum through actual on-site explorations.

Guest Speaker—Students experience the curriculum through another's explorations.

Inquiry or Experiment—Students investigate answers to questions or solutions to problems through hands-on research or reviews of related literature.

Jigsaw—Students work in single-task work groups to become experts on a topic. Then, one member of each of these groups joins another group to teach the topic to others.

K-W-L-Q—This adds one step to the K-W-L chart designed by Donna Ogle in 1986. The K-W-L-Q version accesses prior knowledge (what do you know?), helps students set goals for their learning (what do you want to know?), provides information for assessing learning (what did you learn?), and allows students to continue exploring a topic or concept after a unit of study is completed (what questions do you still have?).

Learning Log (Journal)—This activity involves writing to learn. Learning logs or journals can be used to measure progress, record new information and understandings, and reflect on events and issues.

Lecture/Presentation—The teacher presents new information to students.

Matrix (Cross-Classification Chart)—A matrix is a grid that organizes information so it can be easily and quickly interpreted. It can be used to help students identify what they know and don't know about a topic, solve problems, make decisions, or examine relationships between and among ideas.

Mind Map—The mind map is a whole-brain method for representing and organizing information visually. Because visual images are more easily accessed from long-term memory, mind mapping can help students conceptualize, process, and remember information. Mind maps can be used as note-taking devices or to rehearse new information.

Note Taking—Students write notes from lectures, presentations, written materials, videos, or other input.

Performance—Students use what they know about a topic to design a performance; for example, students create a script and songs for a musical adaptation of Shakespeare's *Macbeth*.

Prediction—Students predict upcoming events in books they are reading or projects in which they are involved.

Project—Students use what they know about a topic to design a product; for example, students guide tours through a classroom museum of landforms they created.

Questioning—The teacher uses a variety of questions to facilitate student thinking and learning.

ReQuest—ReQuest is an active learning strategy for improving reading comprehension. Instead of the teacher asking the questions, roles reverse and students ask the teacher questions about nonfiction material currently being read. The power of this activity lies in students formulating questions. If they can ask a question about the reading, they demonstrate comprehension.

Role Play or Simulation—Simulation and role-play allow students to demonstrate their understanding, explore their perspectives, and develop deeper understanding by imaginatively experiencing real-world roles and situations that are new to them.

SQ3R (Survey-Question-Read-Recite-Review)—Students process written information, as in a textbook, by doing a quick survey of the headings and graphics, generating questions about what they are about to read, actually reading the selection, reciting new learnings, and reviewing the content of the reading.

Stories or Storytelling—The teacher uses stories to elaborate on new concepts, using common language and experiences to make the concept more understandable. Students can also share stories to exemplify concepts.

T-Chart—Students construct a two-column chart labeled "Looks Like..." and "Sounds Like..." and fill in specific examples related to a skill such as *listening* or *cooperation*, or a concept such as *freedom*. The T-Chart can be expanded to a Y-Chart by adding "Feels Like..." to a Y-shaped, three-part chart.

Think-Pair-Share—Think-pair-share is a cooperative learning strategy that gives students an opportunity to think on their own before sharing ideas with one other person. It tends to be low-risk and increases student interaction with content being learned.

Venn Diagram—A Venn diagram is a graphic organizer consisting of two overlapping circles. To compare and contrast two topics, students note similarities where the circles overlap and differences in the respective, non-overlapping sections of the diagram.

Video Clip—The teacher selects and facilitates viewing of a related video clip to help students visualize new information about a topic.

Worksheet—Students complete a preconstructed page related to the study of a topic.

When determining a goal, a teacher may want to first think through: What will the student be able to do after this lesson? Is it measurable? How might it be measured?

Appendix C: Collaborative Learning

Assigning Students to Groups

Before implementing a learning activity in which students work in groups, it's important to think about how you will group students. One option is to allow students to choose their own groups. For some students, this option may increase their motivation to work. For example, students who have worked together in the past may have developed a sense of themselves as a cooperative "team." They may feel significant satisfaction in being allowed to choose their work buddies, and their ability to work well with these students may allow them to get right down to business.

However, depending on your students' level of experience with working in groups and their understanding of the aims of group work, this option may also cause individual students to be left out or may lead to self-segregation by gender, race/ethnicity, or popularity. As a result, your students may miss opportunities to work with those who are different in some ways than themselves. In addition, if the same students work together consistently, they may fall into comfortable roles, rather than try new ones.

One way to ensure that groups are heterogeneous is to assign students to them. But, because having a say in the design of their learning experiences is important to students and can help engage them in their learning activities, you will likely want to allow students to choose their groups at least sometimes. At other times, you may wish to use a random method for choosing groups—such as a counting procedure. For example, if your class-size is 25, and students will work in groups of five, have them count-off from 1 to 5, then ask all "ones" to assemble in a group, all "twos" in another, and so on.

A Note on Heterogeneous Groups

Heterogeneous work groups can provide students with opportunities to work with students from varied backgrounds. When creating heterogeneous work groups, you may wish to consider the following markers of difference, as well as any others you deem important:

- academic skills and ability levels
- gender
- race/ethnicity
- socioeconomic background
- learning styles
- social skills
- self-confidence
- motivation
- popularity

Varying group structure is another way to accustom students to working with students other than those with whom they feel most comfortable. For example, you might allow students to choose their own work groups for an extended project. However, periodically, you could jigsaw students from these groups by creating temporary study groups to accomplish subtasks that support the activity. Similarly, after group work, you could ask students to assemble in mixed discussion groups to share learning or to discuss questions related to the activity. Such arrangements foster student autonomy while also encouraging risk-taking.

Whichever means you choose to assemble groups, it is important to be mindful of group composition across time. No individuals or groups should ever be isolated, disrespected, or neglected as a result of group formation. Rather, all students should have equal access to rich, diverse group experiences and to the learning that accompanies those experiences.

Once you decide the approach you will use, share it with your students. For example, you may want to explain that they will sometimes be permitted to group themselves and that you will sometimes decide how they will be grouped. Emphasize that an important part of group work is learning to work with a variety of people and that groups will be reconfigured frequently.

Diversity Seating

After you introduce students to the value of student diversity and its role in group work, you may wish to consider developing a "diversity" seating chart—one based on students' differences. The goal of your seating arrangement would be to prevent students from clustering according to culture, race/ethnicity, gender, or clique.

Depending on your students' comfort with diversity, you may wish to make this your year-round seating arrangement or to let students choose their own seats at times and use your diversity seating arrangement for special purposes. For example, you could use this type of seating during discussion, or when you want to pair students with others to their right or left to accomplish specific processing goals.

Establishing a Collaborative Code with Students

You can set the stage for this group activity by pointing out to your students that their success with group work depends on their commitment to team behaviors that support collaboration. Begin by explaining that you want the class to work together to establish the behaviors that will support them when they work in groups. Add that, in order to do this, it may help to understand the benefits of group learning. Ask them, "How do you imagine you may benefit from working together?" As students brainstorm, chart their responses and encourage them to collapse similar responses in order to keep the list manageable.

The complexity of your students' code should reflect their grade level and maturity. Dissuade students from including superficial benefits; help them refine such responses by prompting them toward more meaningful answers. It may be helpful to provide an "Examples" column in the chart so that duplicate contributions can be used in some way. Also, the examples may help illuminate the benefits for some students.

Students who are new to group work may need prompting to generate potential benefits. Use questions, or provide scenarios, to elicit additional benefits from students until you feel that all important benefits have been considered. For example, to elicit a benefit about learning from differences, you could ask students, "How might it help you to work with others who are different than you are in some way?"

Sample chart:

Benefits of Group Learning

Benefit	Example
Example: *It teaches students how to work together with different types of people.*	***Example:*** *You could learn how someone else does something and you may want to use that way, too.*

You can set the stage for this group activity by pointing out to your students that their success with group work depends on their commitment to team behaviors that support collaboration.

Sample benefits:

- Gives each student many ***opportunities to contribute to group learning***
- Encourages students to ***share leadership roles***
- Makes learning ***more interesting, meaningful, and relevant*** for students
- Challenges students to ***think more deeply***
- Promotes deeper, ***more memorable understanding***
- Allows students to ***learn from each other*** as well as from the teacher
- Teaches students ***how to work together*** with different types of people
- ***Invites students to challenge and encourage*** each other to think and to take learning risks
- Shows students that their ***diversity enriches their products and performances***

Keep the benefits chart where students can see it. Then, ask students, "What behaviors can help you work together effectively?" They will likely have an easier time with this list than the previous one, but again, use questions and scenarios to help students generate and chart behaviors that support group work.

Sample chart:

Supportive Behaviors

Benefit	Example
Example: *Show respect for cultural differences, students' opinions, and students' ideas.*	***Example:*** *Remember no one is "right" when it comes to values and opinions.*

Sample supportive behaviors:

- Share responsibilities fairly.
- Show respect for one another—listen.
- Keep an open mind—be willing to try the ideas of others.
- When you disagree, express your ideas but don't attack others.
- When someone disagrees with you, don't take it personally.
- Strive for consensus when making decisions.
- Stay focused on group goals.
- Always do your personal best.
- Cooperate—help others succeed and ask for help when you need it.
- Take risks—push yourself to try new roles and greater challenges.
- Be sure the group product represents the contributions of all group members.
- Take pride in working well as a team.

The time you choose to develop a collaborative code with your students can also be a good time to explain how your role will change during group work. For example, you may want to let students know that you plan to provide them with structured, interesting activities they can accomplish, and that as they work in groups, you will offer ongoing feedback and support. Letting students know that even though they will be working independently, they will not be working alone—that you will be there to provide assistance and resources to help them succeed—may calm their fears about succeeding with your new approach.

After establishing a collaborative code with your students, return to it periodically as a means of asking the class to assess its success with group work. For example, after telling the class, "Now that you have some experience with group work, let's review our collaborative code," you could ask them:

- "Which behaviors and attitudes are most important?"
- "Which behaviors and attitudes are most difficult to achieve?"
- "With which behaviors and attitudes are we most successful?"
- "Is our code still appropriate for our needs?"
- "Are there behaviors and attitudes we can add to reach a higher level of success?"

Be sure to remind students not to mention the behavior of specific students during such discussions, but to speak generally. If the class is struggling to control negative behaviors, you may also want to ask each student to write a personal goal for him/herself that he or she will not be required to share with the class.

Helping Students Manage Group Work

As you monitor group work, you will likely find numerous opportunities to encourage, redirect, and reinforce students' group-process skills. In addition, you can enlist students in monitoring how they function in teams. The list that follows describes some possible roles students may play to help manage their group work. These roles and others can be divided or combined depending on the number of students who are working together and on students' experience with group work.

- **Facilitator:** The Facilitator uses interpersonal skills to help students work together and to keep the group on task. She or he facilitates group decision making, makes certain each group member completes his or her task, and looks out for the success of all group members.
- **Reporter:** The Reporter's job is to document group decisions and discussions by taking notes. When needed, the Reporter presents the group's decisions or opinions to the class either verbally or in writing.
- **Timer:** The Timer makes sure that the group accomplishes its task in the time allotted. Once the group determines its course of action, the Timer helps the group set goals to accomplish the work in steps and on a schedule. The Timer then monitors how well the group sticks to its schedule. If the group has difficulty meeting its schedule, the Timer informs the teacher.
- **Fact Checker:** The Fact Checker confirms that the group's products actually represent all of the efforts and opinions of its members. The Fact Checker can also be asked to verify the accuracy of information used by the group, as it is represented in the group's final product.
- **Tutor:** The Tutor provides assistance when other students in the group need help understanding content or applying skills.
- **Researcher:** The Researcher locates information and resources the group needs to complete its work. (If an activity has a strong research component, more than one student may be needed to play this role or all students may need to conduct some research.)
- **Questioner:** The Questioner acts as a go-between for the group when students are unsure about how to proceed. She or he takes the group's queries to the teacher, or surveys other groups, to get answers to the group's questions.

It's important to discuss group roles with students before assigning them for the first time and to introduce them gradually. (For information on group role discussion, see: Collins, M. (2003), *Engaging students in learning,* p. 110-111, Princeton, NJ: ETS.) When you do, emphasize the value of rotating roles fairly so that each student in the group has an equal opportunity to develop skill with that role. Initially, you may wish to maintain the composition of groups for a few weeks so that each student has a chance to play multiple roles and each team has sufficient opportunities to bond.

Periodically, invite students to evaluate their success with these management roles and to share ideas for performing effectively in specific roles. For example, after telling the class, "Now that you have each had some experience with different group roles, let's talk about how well they are working for you," you could ask them:

- "Which roles are most demanding?"
- "How does each role contribute to the group's success?"
- "Can anyone suggest ways to perform these roles more effectively?"
- "Are there other roles that might help us achieve a higher level of success?"

Other Grouping Considerations

When creating cooperative learning groups, consider some of the following student characteristics:

- academic skills and ability levels
- gender
- cultural heritage
- race/ethnicity
- family background
- socioeconomic background
- social skills
- level of self-confidence
- level of motivation
- leadership skills
- learning needs and preferences
- interests, hobbies, passions

Notes

Notes

Many of the sources referenced below from the National Board for Professional Teaching Standards (NBPTS) are available through this organization's Web site at ***http://www.nbpts.org/candidates/guide/downloads.html***.

Many of the sources referenced below from Educational Testing Service (ETS) are available through this organization's Web site at ***http://www.ets.org/pathwise***.

Introduction

1 The Overview was adapted/reprinted with permission of the publisher from (a) *NBPTS Assessor Training Manual,* (Arlington, VA, NBPTS, 2004), 1-2, and (b) *The Guide to Preparing your "Profile of Professional Growth,"* (Arlington, VA, NBPTS, 2004), 1.

2 Adapted/reprinted with permission of the publisher from *Middle Childhood Generalist Portfolio* (Arlington, VA, NBPTS, 2003), 44-47. This material can also be found on the *NBPTS Middle Childhood Generalist Certificate* CD-ROM.

3 Adapted/reprinted with permission of the publisher from (a) *Framework Observation Program: Participant Guidebook* (Princeton, NJ, ETS, 2001), 25, and (b) M. Collins, *Understanding Standards-based Assessment: Resource Book* (Princeton, NJ, ETS, In Press).

4 Adapted/reprinted with permission of the publisher from *NBPTS Assessment and Scoring Kit* (Arlington, VA, NBPTS, 2004), tab 6, p. 3.

Stage 1: Identify

Except where noted, the material in Stage 1 was adapted/reprinted with permission of the publisher from D. Baer, *Demonstrating Knowledge of Students* (Princeton, NJ, ETS, 2003).

1 The contents of the Next Steps section and the introduction of the Learning Goals section of Stage 1 were adapted/reprinted with permission of the publisher from *Understanding Early Literacy Learning: Facilitator's Kit* (Princeton, NJ, ETS, 2003).

2 Adapted/reprinted with permission of the publisher from *Framework Portfolio Program: Components of Professional Practice Booklet* (Princeton, NJ, ETS, 2001), 14-15. This booklet is based on work Charlotte Danielson did at ETS on Praxis III and the NBPTS teaching standards. The framework for teaching is aligned with the Interstate New Teachers Assessment and Support Consortium (INTASC) and NBPTS Standards.

3 Adapted/reprinted with permission of the publisher from *Framework Observation Program: Leader Notes* (Princeton, NJ, ETS, 2001), 79, 81.

4 This learning activity was adapted/reprinted with permission of the publisher from *Framework Observation Program: Participant Guidebook,* (Princeton, NJ, ETS, 2001), 47.

5 Adapted with permission of the publisher from *Understanding Early Literacy Learning Facilitator's Kit* (Princeton, NJ, ETS, 2003).

Stage 2: Plan

Except where noted, the contents of Stage 2 were adapted/reprinted with permission of the publisher from B.P. Murray, *Designing Coherent Instruction* (Princeton, NJ, ETS, 2003).

1 Portions of the *What is Coherent Instruction?* section of Stage 2 were adapted/reprinted with permission of the publisher from M. Collins, *Engaging Students in Learning* (Princeton, NJ, ETS, 2003).

2 Portions of the Learning Activities section in Stage 2 were adapted/reprinted with permission of the publisher from (a) *NBPTS Middle Childhood Generalist Standards* (2nd ed.) (Arlington, VA, NBPTS, 2001); (b) *NBPTS Early Adolescence Science Standards* (2nd ed.) (Arlington, VA, NBPTS, 2003); and (c) *NBPTS Early and Middle Childhood Literacy: Reading-Language Arts Standards* (Arlington, VA, NBPTS, 2002).

3 For tips on team-building activities and collaboration, see M. Collins, *Engaging Students in Learning* (Princeton, NJ, ETS, 2003).

4 Adapted/reprinted with permission of the publisher from M. Collins, *Engaging Students in Learning* (Princeton, NJ, ETS, 2003).

5 The introduction to the *It's Your Turn* activity was adapted/reprinted with permission of the publisher, from *Understanding Early Literacy Learning Facilitator's Kit* (Princeton, NJ, ETS, 2003).

Stage 3: Implement

1 Adapted/reprinted with permission of the publisher from *Early Adolescence English Language Arts Standards* (Arlington, VA, NBPTS, 2001), 19, and *Middle Childhood Generalist Portfolio* (Arlington, VA, NBPTS, 2003), 23.

2 Adapted/reprinted with permission of the publisher from *Framework Portfolio Program: Components of Professional Practice Booklet* (Princeton, NJ ETS, 2001), 24-33.

3 Adapted/reprinted with permission of the publisher from *Framework Observation Program: Teaching Profile* (Princeton, NJ, ETS, 2001).

4 Adapted/reprinted with permission of the publisher from I. Skolnik, *Managing Student Behavior* (Princeton, NJ, ETS, 2003).

5 Adapted/reprinted with permission of the publisher from M. Collins, *Engaging Students in Learning* (Princeton, NJ, ETS, 2003).

6 Adapted/reprinted with permission of the publisher from M. Collins, *Engaging Students in Learning* (Princeton, NJ, ETS, 2003).

7 Adapted/reprinted with permission of the publisher from *Middle Childhood Generalist Portfolio* (Arlington, VA, NBPTS, 2003), Getting Started, 38-39.

8 Adapted/reprinted with permission of the publisher from M. Collins, *Understanding Standards-based Assessment: Resource Book* (Princeton, NJ, ETS, In press).

Stage 4: Analyze and Interpret

1 Adapted with permission of the publisher from *Middle Childhood Generalist Portfolio* (Arlington, VA, NBPTS, 2003), Getting Started, 13-14.

2 Adapted/reprinted with permission of the publisher from B.P. Murray, *Designing Coherent Instruction* (Princeton, NJ, ETS, 2003).

3 Ibid, Stage 4, 2.

4 Questions 1 and 2 of this activity were adapted/reprinted with permission of the publisher from B.P. Murray, *Designing Coherent Instruction* (Princeton, NJ, ETS, 2003).

5 Questions 3-6 were adapted/reprinted with permission of the publisher from *NBPTS Early Adolescence Math Portfolio* (Arlington, VA, NBPTS, 2004), 177.

6 Questions 7-8 were adapted/reprinted with permission of the publisher from *Framework Portfolio Program* (Princeton, NJ, ETS, 2001), Inquiry 3, Form F.

Stage 5: Reflect and Apply

1 Adapted/reprinted with permission of the publisher from M. Collins, *Understanding Standards-based Assessment: Resource Book* (Princeton, NJ, ETS, In Press).

2 Questions 1-5 of this activity were adapted/reprinted with permission of the publisher from *Framework Observation Program: Reflection Questions* (Princeton, NJ, ETS, 2001). Questions 6 and 8 were adapted/reprinted with permission of the publisher from *Framework Portfolio Program* (Princeton, NJ, ETS 2001), Inquiry 3, Form F. Questions 1, 7, and 9 were adapted/reprinted with permission of the publisher from *Early Adolescence English Language Arts Portfolio* (Arlington, VA, NBPTS, 2001), Entry 3, 176.

3 Ibid., Stage 5, 1.

Conclusion

1 Adapted/reprinted with permission of the publisher from *Early Childhood Generalist Scoring Guide* (Arlington, VA, NBPTS, 2001), Background Information, 16.

2 Adapted/reprinted with permission of the publisher from *Early Adolescence through Young Adulthood: World Languages Other than English. Scoring Guide*, (Arlington, VA, NBPTS, 2003), Entry 2: Building Communicative and Cultural Competence, 27-34.

3 Adapted/reprinted with permission of the publisher from *Framework Observation Program: Participant Guidebook,* (Princeton, NJ, ETS, 2001), 25.

4 Adapted/reprinted with permission of the publisher from *Early Adolescence through Young Adulthood: World Languages Other than English. Scoring Guide,* (Arlington, VA, NBPTS, 2002), Entry 2: Building Communicative and Cultural Competence, 27-34.

5 Adapted/reprinted with permission of the publisher from M. Collins, *Engaging Students in Learning* (Princeton, NJ, ETS, 2003), 158.

Appendices:

Appendix A was adapted/reprinted with permission of the publisher from D. Baer, *Demonstrating Knowledge of Students,* (Princeton, NJ, ETS, 2003).

Appendix B was adapted/reprinted with permission of the publisher from B.P. Murray, *Designing Coherent Instruction* (Princeton, NJ, ETS, 2003).

Appendix C was adapted/reprinted with permission of the publisher from M. Collins, *Engaging Students in Learning* (Princeton, NJ, ETS, 2003).

Notes

Notes

Notes

Notes

Notes

Notes

Notes

Notes